CRAZY
With the Papers
to Prove It

Also by Dan Coughlin:

Pass the Nuts

Let's Have Another

Dan Coughlin

CRAZY

With the Papers to Prove It

Stories About the Most Unusual,
Eccentric and Outlandish People I've Known
in Four Decades as a Sports Journalist

GRAY & COMPANY, PUBLISHERS
CLEVELAND

Gray & Company, Publishers
www.grayco.com

Library of Congress Cataloging-in-Publication Data
Coughlin, Dan.
Crazy, with the papers to prove it : stories about the unusual, eccentric and outlandish people i knew and covered in 45 years as a journalist / Dan Coughlin.
p. cm.
ISBN 978-1-59851-068-3
1. Coughlin, Dan. 2. Sportscasters—United States. 3. Sports—United States—Anecdotes. 4. Sports—Ohio—Cleveland—Anecdotes. 5. Athletes—Ohio—Cleveland—Anecdotes. I. Title.
GV742.42.C68A3 2010
070.449796092—dc22
[B]   2010034620

Printed in the United States of America
2.0

*To Maddy for urging me to quit
wasting time and write the book.
Then she grew impatient when I
spent too much time on the book.
Sometimes you can't win.
To Joe, John, Mike and Mary
for taking my side.*

Contents

Introduction

It was one of the happiest days of my life. I was honorably discharged from the U.S. Army at Fort Hood, Texas, having attained the rank of private, and I was returning to my real life as a newspaper reporter.

I shot at nobody and nobody shot at me during my quiet two years with the First Armored Division. It was the Cold War, in between Korea and Viet Nam. Troops returning from Viet Nam in the early 1960s extolled the pleasure of that little civil war. American soldiers, mostly sergeants, were advisors who went out on patrol in the morning with the South Vietnamese troops and by five o'clock they were showered and shaved and snuggled up to the bar of their Saigon hotel. They lived like gentlemen. Maids cleaned their rooms, ironed their clothes and polished their boots. Many of my friends, all of us cynical two-year draftees mired in the monotony of central Texas, said we wanted to go there.

"That's the way to fight a war," we agreed.

But to get that prize, we had to extend our hitch to a third year and none of us would do it. So there we stagnated, cleaning our rifles and building crummy little bridges over a crummy little river. We were there to balance the teeter-totter. The U.S. had to have as many troops in uniform as the Soviets and the Chinese. Here's what this worldwide balancing act meant to me. I went from 75 bucks a week on a small newspaper to 75 bucks a month plus food and lodging. This was not my idea of balance.

As I said, there was no shooting, although we did come close. During the Cuban Missile Crisis in October 1962, the First Armored Division was dispatched to Fort Stewart, Georgia, for the invasion of Cuba. If we were the Army's most battle-ready division, a random collection of inert draftees, God help us.

All of our equipment was transported on railroad flatcars after the markings were painted over. The 15,000 troops went by plane. Mine, a pastel blue Boeing 707 chartered from Braniff Airlines, left at four o'clock in the morning from Waco Airport. We boarded with rifles slung over our shoulders or pistols on our hips and even with

50-caliber machine guns in the aisles. At the top of the steps a stewardess said, "Welcome to Braniff Airlines."

A month later, after the Soviet Union agreed to dismantle its missiles in Cuba and we agreed to close two U.S. missile installations in Turkey, the invasion was cancelled. We returned to Texas on a troop train and resumed counting time.

All this time I was writing letters to newspapers and some of them actually wrote back. Among them was the *St. Louis Post-Dispatch*. The managing editor said he had an opening for a general assignment reporter and he agreed to interview me. We set up the interview for the day after I was discharged. The interview was scheduled for two o'clock in the afternoon of Nov. 22, 1963, a Friday.

Thursday afternoon we drove north through Texas in Bob Schweitzer's 1956 Chevy. There were no interstates. Our highway took us right through Dallas, past Dealey Plaza and the Texas School Book Depository. We never gave it a second look. We left Texas in the rear view mirror as we crossed into Oklahoma and on to Missouri. At six o'clock in the morning Schweitzer dropped me off at the Statler Hotel in downtown St. Louis.

"Good luck, Bob," I said as I pulled my duffle bag out of the trunk of his Chevy. "Stay in touch. You can reach me at the *Post-Dispatch*."

He waved and continued east. He was a forest ranger. I haven't seen him since.

Noontime programming on St. Louis television was a lady playing the piano. I had just gotten out of the shower when an off-screen voice interrupted her.

"President Kennedy has been shot in Dallas," the voice said.

I felt as though I had taken the bullet. I remember vividly what I thought. "Damn. Damn. Damn. My interview will be cancelled." I clinched first prize for selfishness at that moment.

Of course, it was cancelled. Everything was cancelled that week except for the National Football League. NFL commissioner Pete Rozelle always regretted playing the games. Every college game was cancelled that weekend. Television schedules were interrupted. Stores were closed. I spoke on the phone with the managing editor's secretary and we agreed that in a few days I would call and reschedule the interview. I flew home to Cleveland on Saturday and we all settled in to watch the Kennedy drama unfold on television, bullet by bullet.

After the twelve o'clock Mass at St. Clement's Catholic Church in Lakewood that Sunday I ran into an old family friend, J. Ralph Novak, whom everybody called Sarge. He was an old newspaper reporter who still knew everything that was happening in that business.

"*The Plain Dealer* will have an opening in sports," he said. "I know Gordon Cobbledick. I'll call him for you."

I grew up reading Cobbledick, who was a legendary sports editor and columnist. I never applied to *The Plain Dealer*. Surely that was beyond my reach. I tried to keep my goals realistic. But with "Sarge" Novak's encouragement, I called Cobbledick and he invited me to his office for an interview. What a courteous gentleman! I was the last person he hired before he retired. At the *St. Louis Post-Dispatch* they're still waiting for me to reschedule our interview.

Nowadays when kids ask about finding a job, I tell them a good place to start is at church.

Forty years later I learned that I had taken the job of a friend. In 2004 Tom Brazaitis wrote a series of columns on *The Plain Dealer* op-ed page about his battle with cancer. He was dying. In one of them he reflected on his ambition to write sports for *The Plain Dealer*. He had worked part time on the high school sports staff when he was in college at John Carroll. He had a foot in the door and he was led to believe he had a job waiting for him when he was discharged from the army. I never knew that. When he got home, he discovered that I had his job. Tom edited the *East Cleveland Leader*, his hometown weekly, for about 10 years and then joined *The Plain Dealer* where he rose to Washington bureau chief. He was a smart guy. I would say he did nicely. Sadly, he died on March 30, 2005.

* * *

The next four decades were the answer to my prayers. Lou Gehrig wasn't the luckiest guy on the face of the earth. I was. For 18 years I enjoyed the last great era of old-time newspapering. Circulation and advertising increased every year. It was as though hundred dollar bills were flying off the presses. The reporters didn't see many of them, but there were other tradeoffs. They tolerated our eccentricities.

When I signed on, *The Plain Dealer* had hired a lot of aggressive young reporters. There was a sizzle in the city room. I was thrilled to be part of it. Anyone who did not have a good time at *The Plain Dealer* wasn't trying. Lord, I loved it.

I was there for the change. Newspapers once were mom and pop operations. Owners kept their distance. By 1980 they started to get corporate. Technology eliminated jobs and then entire newspapers were eliminated. The bulldog edition was replaced by the mouse.

For the next 25 years I caught the last fun days of radio and television. The newsroom at WJW-TV was like Cedar Point except the lines were shorter. It was loud and raucous. We were dominant and we were cocky. We had money and we spent it. For example, when big stories broke, we invaded with three reporters, two cameramen and a producer. When we covered high school football, we covered it like the Super Bowl. We flew to distant games in a helicopter, the Cadillac of the air, a four-person craft with room for a reporter, cameraman and intern. Tony Rizzo said that when he landed next to a high school field, he felt like a rock star.

Eventually, the music stopped. We went from a 40 rating at six o'clock to a six or seven. I had that old familiar feeling. Newspapers went corporate, then they went Internet and then they went out of business. Television went cable and then it went You Tube and then it went viewer participation. The media turned into a hobby, like growing roses. Citizen journalists just kept spreading more fertilizer on the flowers and there was no shortage of fertilizer.

In the summer of 2009 I rode off into the sunset with wild and exotic memories of bizarre characters and events in my saddle bag. Thank God I'm still around to share them with you.

Junior O'Malley: He Died a Thousand Deaths

My first duties at *The Plain Dealer* in January 1964 were menial but important. Bookies and gamblers depended on me, especially in the winter when Thistledown Racetrack was dark. That's when horse players turned their attention to out of town tracks such as Aqueduct in New York, Arlington Park in Chicago, Hialeah in Miami, Laurel in Baltimore and the Fairgrounds in New Orleans.

Each afternoon I assembled the race results from all over the country as they rattled out of the *Associated Press* teletype machine, unfurling from rolls like toilet paper. I pasted them together, rolled them up in plastic vacuum tubes and zoomed them to the composing room to be set in agate type.

A bank of *Associated Press* printers clattered away in a neat row behind the sports copy desk. There was the Ohio sports wire, the national sports wire, the racing wire and the Western Union printer. They were never turned off. They ran all day and all night. In the morning, teletype copy would be coiled in piles on the floor. The rhythmic clackety-clack of the machines gave the sports department its pulse, even when nobody was there, which was usually the case in mid-afternoon before the copy editors got to work and before the reporters and rewrite men wandered in.

About three o'clock every day a beefy, middle-aged man with *The Daily Racing Form* poking out of the right pocket of his black cashmere overcoat bustled through the sports department and headed for the race wire, directly under the crudely drawn "No Loitering" sign that hung by a string from the ceiling. He leaned over it, he hugged it, caressing the copy through his hands as it emerged from the teletype machine in starts and stops. He spoke not a word. Then, as abruptly as he had arrived, he hurried away toward the middle of the city room and disappeared up the steps leading to the composing room.

And so began my 30-year adventure with Junior O'Malley, the most degenerate horse player in the Eastern Time zone.

*   *   *

Junior began taking me to Thistledown. The first time he marked my program, telling me what horses to bet. He marked all 10 races and he did not pick a single winner.

"Do you realize how hard that is?" he said. "It's not easy."

It turned out that Junior and I were almost related. Our families grew up together in St. Rose's Parish on Cleveland's west side. Some people pretend to be worried about inbreeding among the Irish on the west side. We're like little West Virginia. My cousin Eileen Griffin says we're one generation away from turning out kids with one eye in the middle of their foreheads. For example, Eileen is my first cousin. She is married to the second cousin of my wife's mother. I challenge you to diagram that. Get ready to celebrate the first Cyclops born at Fairview General Hospital.

Junior worked as a proofreader at *The Plain Dealer*, a high-paying union job. As a matter of fact, his grandfather was once president of the Typographical Union in Cleveland. But Junior's heart was at the racetrack. When Thistledown opened in the spring, he took a leave of absence from the paper and worked as a mutuel clerk at the racetrack for half the pay.

He couldn't resist a bet. In the 1960s he learned of a crap game in a barn in Medina County. He was out there the next night.

"You had to climb a ladder to the hayloft," Junior recalled. "But once you got up there, it was pretty plush. They had it fixed up real nice. They cleaned up all the hay. Well, I get in this crap game and I'm going hot and heavy and before long I lost two or three-hundred dollars, everything I had. Leo the Lip, who ran the game, took me aside and gave me back all my money. 'Get out of here,' Leo said. 'The game is rigged.' Pretty soon he sees me right back at the table, betting just as strong as before. He got me aside again and said, 'Don't you understand what I told you? It's a crooked game.' I heard him the first time. 'But it's the only game in town,' I said."

Like most degenerate gamblers, he paraphrased Grantland Rice: "It isn't whether you win or lose, but if you're in the game."

A good crap game, on the level or not, was irresistible, but Junior's true compulsion was the racetrack. He admits that he once bet on a race he knew was fixed and he picked the loser.

Nevertheless, he enjoyed a reputation as a savvy judge of horse-flesh because he occasionally scored big and when he won, everybody won. If he cashed a $900 ticket, he spent a thousand celebrating in the bar that night. An occasional triumph was inevitable because he bet every race every day of his life. He never conceded one. He never said, "This one is impossible to handicap." What he did say was, "There's a winner in every race and I'm gonna find it."

He once said to me, "Let me show you my $12,000 bottle of whisky," whereupon he held up a bottle of VO, top shelf stuff, but hardly worth $12,000.

"A Christmas present from my bookie," he said.

Junior once claimed that the only reason he gambled was to give his wife, Didie, a better life.

"It cost me $5,000 to buy her a $700 dining room set," he said.

Didie worked for 20 years as the secretary to the mutuel director at Thistledown. Here was the difference between them. Didie actually took home her take-home pay.

Junior and Didie had their first date on St. Patrick's Day, 1939.

"He got drunk," said Didie.

The next day the police swooped in to arrest Junior on a long-standing assault and battery charge.

"He's a bad one," said Didie's mother.

Four months later they were married.

"It will never last," said Didie's mother.

"Let me be the first to offer my condolences," Junior's father said to Didie.

It lasted for 44 years. She married Junior for better or worse and she had plenty of both.

*   *   *

Junior's love affair with horses began with his baptism in 1915 when he was about a month old. His father borrowed the milkman's horse so that Junior and his mother, Ruby, could ride to St. Rose's Church in a carriage.

As Junior heard the story years later, the horse was white. The night before the christening Junior's father and his cronies got drunk and decided that for the first-born child of an Irish family, the horse should be green.

"So they painted the poor devil. They painted him green," Junior said.

Erasing original sin from the soul of baby James Francis Aloysius O'Malley proved to be much easier than erasing the green paint from the hide of Old Dobbin.

"They used turpentine," Junior said. "When they hit him with the turpentine, he bolted and raced down Detroit Avenue from West 116th Street to West 110th in thirty-two and two-fifths seconds, still a track record for Detroit Avenue. The Humane Society had my father arrested. Horses have been getting even with me ever since."

From the day Junior was embraced by Holy Mother Church, his life took on new meaning. He failed to survive the eighth grade at St. Rose's School, having been expelled by Father O'Connell for reading *The Daily Racing Form* while his classmates were studying the Baltimore Catechism. Asked about Baltimore, Junior said, "That's where they run the Preakness."

"Sister Gilbert caught me reading the *Racing Form*. She was horrified and took me to the principal, Sister Agnes, who took me right up the chain of command. She took me to Father O'Connell, the pastor. Father O'Connell asked me what the *Racing Form* was. He had never seen one. So I said, 'See, Father. Take this horse. He was third at the quarter and fifth at the half . . .' Just then he hauled off and let me have it, right in the kisser.

"Next in line to see Father O'Connell was your uncle, Frank Coughlin, who was up on another rap," Junior said to me. "When he saw Father O'Connell whack me, he was terrified. He went running down the hall screaming, 'It's a curse to get hit by a priest.'

"Turns out he was right," Junior continued. "How else can you explain it? Every day I go out there bruised and bloodied and instead of cashing tickets, Father O'Connell unloads on me. It's my penance."

Father O'Connell must have been doing something right. He was later promoted to monsignor. Junior, on the other hand, was not promoted to the ninth grade.

*   *   *

Out of school and out of money, Junior followed his passion, a journey that took him to Bainbridge Park, a small racetrack in Geauga County near Cleveland that prospered in the 1920s and '30s.

"I was 14 years old but I had the run of the place because Tommy McGinty owned a piece of the track and I would drive Mrs. McGinty out there each day. Well, my father was out of work. We had no food in the house. We had no money. It was 1929 and the Depression was ready to start. My father was already depressed when he saw the hungry looks on the faces of my mother, my sister and me. He said that if he had $2 he would go to the racetrack and try to parlay it into enough to buy some food.

"I told him my Aunt Peg had put $7 in a savings account for me at the Cleveland Trust on Detroit Avenue. The money was still there because Tip O'Neill hadn't robbed the bank yet. After he robbed it we always called it Tip's bank.

"My father had an old Chevrolet. We got the $7 and drove out to Bainbridge Racetrack. My father knew I was friendly with a lot of the kids who worked in the stables. He told me to go back there and get some information. My friend Danny worked for an owner who had a cheap horse named Erin Go Bragh. He wasn't much of a horse, but Danny told me that on a heavy track this horse could not lose and the track that day was real heavy.

"We were chiseling up and down, betting to show, and we were down to $5. My father gave me $2 and said bet Erin Go Bragh to place. He wanted to play it safe. He kept thinking of my mother and sister at home waiting for food. I pleaded with him to bet Erin Go Bragh to win. I begged. He relented. Instead of $2, he gave me $4 and I bet it right on Erin Go Bragh's nose. He was 25 to one.

"The race starts and Erin Go Bragh was last by 20 lengths. They go into the first turn and he's last by 30 lengths. I started to cry. My father and I started to walk away. Then we heard the track announcer shout, 'Here comes Erin Go Bragh. Look at that horse run.'

"Well, he wins and pays $52 so we've got $104. My father bets another horse and he pays $20. Now we have more money than my father has seen in three months. That night we went out and had a big dinner at the fanciest restaurant on the west side. My father paid off some markers. It brightened his outlook. It changed his life. Six years later my father and Jake Price, who later owned Carry Back, were co-owners of the Artesian Club."

At age 14 Junior was finished with school but he continued his education at Bainbridge Racetrack.

"I was hanging around the judges' stand. I heard one judge say, 'Did you see that jockey throw something into the infield?' Another judge said, 'It must have been a battery.' So they called over Toots Washington, who was the general handyman. 'Toots, go out and get that battery,' they told him."

Batteries were racing's version of burglar's tools. They helped a devious jockey steal a purse. These were not your ordinary flashlight batteries. Small but powerful, they could be concealed underneath a rider's racing silks. When the jockey wanted to get the horse's attention, he touched him on the neck with the battery and gave him a few volts. Horses are very responsive to electrical shocks. A battery will make an ordinary claimer feel like Seattle Slew.

"Toots must have gone out and taken a look, because he went back in a barn and got a bushel basket," Junior continued. "Old Toots came back and said, 'Which one do you want, Judge?' It was like batteries were growing out there. After each race the jockeys would gallop their horses around the first turn and toss their batteries over the fence into the infield. Batteries were once as common as manure around a racetrack.

"They can't do that today. They've got patrol judges around the track and video tape replays with three cameras. If anything looks suspicious, they look at the replay and call down to search the boy's tack when he gets off his horse. They're making it very hard to cheat."

* * *

Junior and Didie had been married only a couple of years when World War II started and Junior found himself in Burma with Merrill's Marauders fighting the Japanese. He had the usual diseases, such as jungle rot and malaria. He remembers his homecoming when the war was over. He got off the train at the Terminal Tower with his mustering out pay in his pocket. He had about $700.

"That was more money than I had ever seen in my life," he said. "I felt like a millionaire. But I made one big mistake. I stopped in a bookie joint at 12th and Superior to bet a couple of horses."

Within four hours he was broke and despondent. At times such as this a man's religious faith is strongest. His next stop was around the corner at St. John's Cathedral. At that time Catholic Churches were like bars in New Orleans. There were no locks on the doors. They never closed.

"Help! I want to see a priest," Junior bellowed as he barged through the front door. That was like shouting "Fire" in a fire station. Priests, monsignori and auxiliary bishops came running.

"I want to take the pledge," said Junior.

One priest stepped up and took charge. The others slipped away to their prayerful duties.

"You're a drinking man, are you?" asked the priest.

"Of course," said Junior. "But that isn't the problem."

The priest was puzzled. "What is the problem?"

"Horses," said Junior. "I'm addicted to them."

According to Irish Catholic tradition, "The Pledge" is a vow usually associated with abstinence from alcohol. The penalty for breaking such a vow is eternal damnation, an endless dance on hot coals, which is enough to scare the demons out of even the most incorrigible rounder. The priest insisted that Junior's wife be present for such a serious commitment. And so Junior took the bus home to West Boulevard and Clifton, to the home he had not seen in four years. What a bizarre reunion that must have been. He walked in the front door, kissed his wife hello, grabbed her by the arm and dragged her right back downtown on the bus. In the presence of a priest, in the seat of Roman Catholicism in Cleveland, under the same roof as the archbishop, Junior placed his hand on the Bible and swore he never would bet another horse as long as he lived.

News of Junior's homecoming spread throughout the city, but so did rumors about the pledge, causing no small amount of anguish to bookmakers and the local racetracks. The word was slower to reach Maryland, however, where a trainer, an old friend of Junior's, called him with a tip from Pimlico Racetrack.

"It was a sure thing and I needed the money. I called the priest and told him he had to get me off the hook. He had to release me from the pledge," said Junior.

"No," said the priest. "It's not right. You took a vow for life."

"We've got only 45 minutes to post time," Junior urgently told the priest. "I'll be right down to see you."

Junior supplicated himself. He fell to his knees at the same spot where he had taken the pledge one month before. The priest remained adamant.

"If you don't release me from the pledge, you'll make a Protestant out of me," Junior cried. "Besides, I'll cut you in for a sawbuck."

The priest recoiled at such blasphemy but relented.

"James, you are released from your pledge, but we are both going to hell," he said.

"I'm not saying the race was fixed, but the horse won and paid $19. I cut the priest in for $85 for the poor box and made a bundle myself," said Junior.

The lifetime pledge lasted four weeks. To his dying day, however, Junior believed he was haunted by its echo.

"I ain't had any luck ever since," he lamented.

* * *

Due to his grandfather's influence Junior became a printer's apprentice—a printer's "devil" they were called in the trade—but he spent more time at the track betting horses than setting type at the paper, which led to a full-time job as a mutuel clerk at the track. He was there for all the great moments in Thistledown history. A man once collapsed of a heart attack while standing in line to make a bet. A crowd gathered around him.

"Is he still alive?" someone asked.

"Only in the double," said a man looking at the daily double tickets in the dead man's hand.

"We're a hardy breed," Junior always said. "We die a thousand deaths before the results are official."

* * *

Mutuel clerks are the business end of horse racing and Junior's best customer often was himself. He operated like Wall Street in the 1920s. He made bets on margin.

"I would sometimes borrow the track's money, but I was an honest crook," Junior insisted. "Back then, they would come around and collect our money after each race. Well, I was $2 short after the first race and $10 short after the second race."

It would be fine if Junior's horses won. He could cover his bets with the money he won. No harm, no foul. But if he lost, the track would make up the difference in the mutuel pool and no one was happy.

Mutuel manager Bob Sloan had sent word to the money counting room that he was to be told immediately if Junior was even $2 short. Junior was already over his limit and the third race hadn't even gone off.

"Now I'm punching tickets on the third race. I had people lined up at my window and I'm ignoring them. I was punching my own tickets," he said.

Word spread up and down the main line, from window to window, like a California brushfire. The entire plant was in a panic. Alarms sounded, bells rang, sirens went off.

"Word reached Sloan and he came out running. He rushed up just as the race went off. I had punched out $700 in tickets. He said, 'What horse did you bet?' I told him number seven. He said, 'You're fired.' And he's snapping his fingers. 'C'mon seven.' Well, number seven wins and Mr. Sloan grabs my tickets and the money in my box and I said, 'Don't get your money mixed up with mine.' As usual, they suspended me for two weeks."

* * *

Junior had the wanderlust sometimes. He and Didie traveled from city to city, working on newspapers located near racetracks. They were called "tramp printers." He worked at the *Cincinnati Enquirer* because of its proximity to River Downs and it was there that he became friendly with another horse-loving printer named Robert Chutjian, whose difficult Armenian name baffled Junior. The closest Junior could come was "Shotgun."

After a successful afternoon at River Downs, Junior and Chutjian partied through the night and into the morning, leaving their winnings and what was left of their last paychecks in an after-hours joint in Covington, Kentucky. Hungry, thirsty and broke, they stumbled into the composing room of the *Enquirer* in search of a loan. Their timing could not have been worse. Early in the morning there was only a skeleton shift of printers on duty. Furthermore, it was the day before payday. One printer, however, took pity on them. He wrote out a personal check for $20, enough to get them jump-started that day at the Downs.

"Just a minute," said their benefactor. "You guys look like hell. You haven't shaved. Your clothes are rumpled. No bank will cash a personal check for you guys. Take this note. Go to the bank around the corner. Give the note to the first teller. He knows me. He'll cash the check."

They were there half an hour before the bank opened, pacing conspicuously back and forth on the sidewalk. When the uniformed security guard unlocked the front doors, these two characters rushed in. Chutjian headed directly toward the third teller.

"Hey, Shotgun," Junior shouted, "give the note to the first teller."

What happened next, Junior said later, was straight out of the movies.

"You should have seen the place go into action. They thought it was a stickup. Out of the corner of my eye, I saw the guard go for

Stella Walsh:
Stella Was a Fella

Stella Walsh couldn't keep her hands off me. Whenever we met, the old Olympic track champion would come on like an octopus, all arms and hands, grabbing and kissing me, her wild platinum blond wig flying in all directions of the compass, much like Norman Bates' mother in "Psycho." I liked her personally, but she was not easy to handle. Despite the age difference, she was stronger than me, tall and lanky, broad shoulders, well-defined muscles, flat belly. She was either an old doll attracted to a younger man or an old man drawn to a younger doll. It turned out she was both, something we discovered after she was murdered.

We became acquainted in July, 1964. She had just moved back home after 15 years in Los Angeles, where she had worked in a plastics plant, coached the company's baseball and basketball teams, formed a women's track team and been married briefly to a former pro rassler named Harry Olson.

She was living with her parents on Clement Avenue in Cleveland's Warsaw neighborhood and was working as a bartender at the Sunrise Café on East 71st Street, where I interviewed her. I felt embarrassed to discover this Olympic legend in such humble circumstances but she was not uncomfortable.

"They like to talk sports in here and I settle their arguments," she said. It was late afternoon and we were the only ones in the bar. Naturally, we talked sports—mostly about her career.

In the 1950s the Helms Foundation named her America's greatest woman athlete of the first half of the century, even though she competed in the Olympics as a Pole. In 1932 she was the fastest woman in the world when she won the 100 meters at the Los Angeles Olympics. Four years later she finished second in the 100 meters in the Berlin Olympics. In that era there was also an alternate cycle of Summer Games for women only and Stella ran the table in the

1930 Women's Olympics in Prague, Czechoslovakia, winning the 60, 100 and 200 meter sprints. In 1934 she won the 60 meters in the Women's Olympics in London.

She was not Stella Walsh running for the United States, however. That was her shortened, Americanized name. She was actually Stanislawa Walasiewicz of Poland. She was five years old when her parents emigrated from Poland in 1913 and it never occurred to them to apply for U.S. citizenship. Such disinterest was unusual in Cleveland's ethnic neighborhoods, which were crowded with immigrants anxious to become official citizens of their new country. Nevertheless, it provided a peek into the simple and unsophisticated home life of the Walasiewicz family. Stella finally became a naturalized U.S. citizen in 1947, when she was 39 years old.

Anyway, there's your capsule summary of Stella Walsh up to the point where she entered my life. My first story about her was the official announcement that she was back home. After that, I was her guy.

With her platinum plume exploding around her head, she would come breezing through the sports department at any time, usually to promote one of her girls track teams, girls basketball teams or girls softball teams. She always coached girls. I was the only man in her life and she wanted more than friendship. She wanted to race me. Every time she stormed through the newsroom, she would chide, cajole and challenge me to a foot race. Good grief! She was 31 years older than me. She had almost completed the circuit from a gold medal to a Golden Buckeye Card. How could I politely decline the challenge? What kind of a cad would humiliate an old lady in a hundred-yard dash?

Stella's frequent unannounced visits were typical of the era. Think of a newspaper as an insane asylum with no locks on the doors. Any registered eccentric could sashay through the front door, ride the elevator to the second floor and parade through the city room. Some interlopers were notoriously crazy and had the papers to prove it. Crazy was normal in those days.

For example, in 1943 a mad Hungarian named Herbert L. Kobrak walked into the office of John S. McCarrens, the publisher of both *The Plain Dealer* and the *Cleveland News*, and pumped three bullets into him. As McCarrens lay dying on the floor, Kobrak put the pistol to his head and blew out his brains.

It would be difficult to do that today. Newspapers have become impenetrable fortresses. Nobody gets inside without a printed invitation and a security clearance. Characters are not welcome. The upside is that nobody's been assassinated lately in a newspaper office. The downside is that nobody laughs, either.

Anyway, I tolerated Stella's provocations to the point of exasperation. I finally said, "Yes, damnit, I'll race you! I'll race you in the hallway right now. I'll race you to the Headliner Bar next door. I'll race you on a track. You pick the time and place."

I never saw Stella so serious. She got back to me. "The Great Race" was run at Cuyahoga Heights High School track with a roaring crowd of 21 teenagers in the stands and photographer Richard T. Conway on the track. I will now quote liberally from my story in the July 13, 1967, edition of *The Plain Dealer*:

"To make things fair," said Stella, "I'll give you a 10-yard head start."

I accepted. This was entirely proper. Stella is a five-time Olympic gold medal winner, holder of dozens upon dozens of records in scores of countries. She trains an hour a day and plays softball at night. The only thing is, Stella is 59 years old.

On the other hand, I am an out-of-shape, overweight, 5-9, 188-pounder, washed up at 28.

Stella went through a rigorous warmup routine. "I can't take a chance of pulling a muscle," she explained. "I must compete in meets in Buffalo and Chicago and Detroit this summer."

"I'm saving everything for the race," I countered.

Despite my 10-yard head start, Stella had all the advantages. She used starting blocks. I had none. She wore a track uniform and track shoes. I wore Bermuda shorts and sneakers with one broken shoestring.

We crouched for the explosion out of the starting blocks. We had all the toys—starting gun, finish tape, two stop watches.

"Bang." I stepped out to a 10-yard lead (the 10 yards she gave me.) Pound, pound, pound, I gobbled up the yardage. Clomp, clomp, clomp, I heard her closing the gap. Gasp, gasp, gasp, I snapped the tape with Stella still three yards behind me.

The clock showed I had covered 90 yards in 10.8 seconds. Stella clipped off 100 yards in 11.3.

dugout and asked them what in the name of Chief Wahoo they were trying to accomplish.

"Everybody's gone. The Rangers are back at their hotel. Why are you still here?" I asked. No one offered an explanation that could be used in the paper but one kid reached from behind the guy in front of him and landed a right cross on my chin. The kid's footwork was lousy. He was off-balance and he had nothing on the punch. He was drunk, for Pete's sake. I shook it off like a mosquito buzzing my face. But I didn't stick around to give him a second chance to plant his feet and get off another shot.

James C. Pravda, 11 years old, was at the game with his grandfather. They were swept up in the crowd of drunks heading up West 3rd Street after the game. Years later he recalled that terrifying night on a blog that he headlined, "A night of survival on the streets of Cleveland." He posted it on Aug. 7, 2007.

Pravda recalled the crush of drunken humanity pushing and squeezing onto a Rapid Transit train at the Terminal Tower.

"For an 11-year-old the sensation of panic was frightening and very real," he wrote.

He recalled it all. The stench of beer and sweat in the crowded car; the condensation on the windows; the vulgarities, swearing and threats; the train creeping west with a crippled motor, barely five miles an hour out of the Terminal Tower and onto the viaduct over the Cuyahoga River; the train stopping halfway across the viaduct; the lights going out; the electric motor overheating; the orange glow underneath the car. "The train is on fire. We're all gonna die," someone screamed in the darkness.

"There is no fire," the driver announced. "The motor turned off automatically when it overheated. They're sending a new train out to get us."

Pravda and his grandfather waited for 45 minutes with the crazy drunks packed like sardines in a tin can. Two rescue trains eventually arrived and they got home safely, although scarred for life.

The next day Indians president Alva T. (Ted) Bonda was peppered with questions when he faced the media. They came from every possible angle. Finally, Bonda threw up his hands and said, "Wait a minute. You're giving beer a bad name."

That shows what a great man Bonda was. He didn't even drink

beer. In fact, he hardly ever took a sip of alcohol. And he stood there like a champion and defended the amber brew.

Critics demanded that the Indians cancel their next two Dime Beer Nights later that season.

"I thought I was going to get fired when we held a meeting in the office after the game," said Jackie York. "Instead he said, 'You and Carl Fazio are going to Milwaukee tomorrow to find out how they run their beer nights. They're the beer experts.'"

The next beer night that season was July 18. The attendance approached 40,000. Security was increased from 50 to 150 police, sheriff's deputies and private stadium force. There were no injuries and no arrests.

The Indians actually had a long history of successful Beer Nights through the 1970s. The first one was on July 5, 1971, a Sunday afternoon. It featured strolling Dixieland bands and plenty of suds. Beer was only a nickel that day. I did a lengthy story about a beer-drinking contest among three renowned imbibers from Lakewood—James (Tubby) Aylward, a softball player; Bob (The Sponge) Thewes, an unemployed ironworker; and Dale (The Tainted Rose) Rosenthal.

Tubby trained by drinking 22 beers while watching Saturday's game on television and drinking 10 more at night while he plotted his strategy. "I have yet to reach my potential," he boasted. He attributed his longevity to drinking half a quart of milk and eating pancakes before going to bed each morning. Rosenthal's personal best was 40 beers in 12 hours. Thewes, more of a sprinter, once drank 35 beers in 2½ hours. Then he passed out.

"I'm good, but these guys are pros," said Tubby.

I stashed them in a private booth in the press box and personally ran a non-stop supply of Genesee to them. Thewes was the champion as they combined to consume over 60 beers in nine innings. The exact number was not available because my official scorer got drunk and lost track. For all I knew, the official scorer was the winner.

Beer and baseball have enjoyed a long relationship. Cot Deal, who was an Indians coach in the early 1970s, recalled that Detroit Tigers manager Bill Norman could drink a case of beer every night on train trips. "He'd set a case at his feet in the men's lounge and drink the entire 24 bottles while telling stories all night," said Deal.

"That's good, but not great if it took him all night," said Tubby.

Ron Penfound, the Indians' public address announcer at the

time, said that his Kenyon College roommate Paul Newman, the actor, was in the elite class.

"I read where he still drinks 30 Budweisers a day," Penfound said.

Maybe he did in 1971 but some time after that I read that Joanne Woodward had reined him in. Wives sometimes do that, which I can say from personal experience. Nevertheless, Newman would have had a wonderful time in his hometown at the first Nickel Beer Day. I think he would have enjoyed watching the game with Tubby, the Sponge and the Tainted Rose.

"After the game we all went to Slim's Locker Room for a few more beers," said Tubby's sister, Karen Aylward. "We had a wonderful time. When Tubby read about the Beer Night riot a few years later, he was very upset. He wondered why they would destroy such a beautiful thing."

But Dime Beer Night lived on in Cleveland for many years. When Jimmy Carter was in the White House, Jackie York brought in the President's controversial beer-drinking brother, Billy, to preside as "grand marshal" over Beer Night.

"Nice guy," Jackie remembered. "He brought his own case of Billy Beer with him."

Fistfighting in the Aisles

After losing to the Minnesota Twins on Thursday, July 26, 1979, the Indians relaxed over a few beers in the clubhouse and then had more time to kill in the airport lounge. The plane was late taking off and was late arriving in Chicago. The boys had a few more beers in the air. On the ground at O'Hare Airport we had to sit on the runway for almost an hour waiting for a gate. The plane was packed. There must have been 200 people aboard, including nuns and priests who were joining a Chicago tour headed to Rome.

Outside, it was a sweltering day. To save the batteries, the pilot dialed down the air conditioning. Inside the plane, the temperature rose.

Suddenly there was a commotion behind me. Two people were tumbling down the aisle, bouncing off the seats and the people in them. Six nuns in full black and white habits and two priests in black clergy regalia put their arms up defensively to ward off the bodies careening past them. As they went past me, I recognized Indians catcher Ron Pruitt and relief pitcher Victor Cruz. They were fistfighting in the aisle.

I don't know if the pilot radioed in a "mayday" call for help or if our turn simply came up, but a gate opened and soon we were in the terminal.

"What was going on?" I asked Pruitt.

"We do that in the bullpen all the time," was his simple explanation.

The Indians were finally showing some fight. At least they had the will. Neither Cruz nor Pruitt had a mark on them, however, so obviously the Indians still couldn't hit.

Poetic License: Bye, Bye Baseball

For many years I was the baseball backup, coming off the bench to pinch hit, but for all of 1978 and 1979 I was full-time on the baseball beat, assigned exclusively to the Indians, home and away, seven days a week, 24 hours a day, sick or well, drunk or sober—a total commitment. I thought of the roles played by the chicken and the pig in making my breakfast of bacon and eggs. The chicken is involved. The pig is committed.

The season began in February and ended in late October. Fifty thousand miles a year. One hundred and fifty nights in hotels. Loneliness and tedium interrupted only by the terror of gut-wrenching deadlines. Two hundred poems a season.

I had stumbled upon a literary trick to brighten my leads. Because baseball is the oldest game in the country—except for horseshoes and fist fighting—I thought an old style of sports writing would be appropriate. Accordingly, I began each game story with four lines of light verse—poetry. It caught on. Readers seemed to enjoy it. It became my trademark. It also was my burden. Try coming up with a four-line poem—in meter, in rhyme and on deadline.

Here are some examples.

> The old Titanic's famous leak
> Was nothing like our losing streak.
> We're sinking in the murky brine.
> The losing streak is now at nine.

> The stillness in the Wigwam grows,
> Adrenalin no longer flows.
> The losing streak has climbed to ten.
> We ask ourselves, 'When will it end?'

> Here's a plan to halt the fall
> And start the Tribe a'winning.

Change the name to blooper ball
And play just seven innings.

You cannot overemphasize
The artistry of that guy Wise.
He plugged the Tribe's titanic leak
And snapped our ten-game losing streak.

Garland got a win at last,
First one since a year has passed.
'Screwball's back,' the man declared.
'Shoulder's fine, it's been repaired.'

His fast ball cut the corners,
His curve ball slashed the plate.
A fabulous two-hitter
For Cleveland hurler Waits.

Toby Harrah's blast was seen
Landing in the left field screen.
Things are looking mighty nice
Now that someone broke the ice.

Teamsters, umps. United flights
All shut down by labor strikes.
Cleveland batters joined this list;
Every time they've swung, they've missed.

This is not great poetry. Simple meters, simple rhymes. Sometimes not even true rhymes, just similar vowel sounds. But may I suggest that you try it when the game just changed in the top of the ninth at 9:45 p.m. in Chicago. That is 10:45 in Cleveland and the deadline for the first final edition is 11 o'clock.

Life is a tradeoff. Covering a major league team is prestigious. Your stories are prominently displayed and you travel the country on an expense account. The amount of money *The Plain Dealer* spent covering sports in those days was mind-boggling. In my day we traveled with the team. We stayed in decent hotels. We were fed at the ballpark before and during games. We joked about it. "We get in free and they pay us for being here," I said when I dragged myself into the Kansas City press box with a fever of 103. Walking pneumonia in the spring was just part of the game. It was automatic. Getting sick on the road was twice as bad as getting sick at home.

"If you're sick, go home," traveling secretary Mike Seghi said sarcastically as I was hacking up a storm on the bus to the ballpark.

We were in Milwaukee. You don't call in sick when you're on the road.

Regardless of the shape you're in, the loneliness of the road can drive you crazy. It's a marathon. It's a death march. It's a battle for survival. You need a friend. You need a companion. I had a team of them. Fortunately, in the '70s I got along easily with my Indians, who formed a nice support group. I reflect wistfully on some of those late night moments in hotel coffee shops—manager Jeff Torborg drinking milk shakes, second baseman Duane Kuiper drinking coffee, broadcaster Joe Tait eating sundaes and me drinking beer.

Back home, however, several bartenders who had children in private schools depended on me. Furthermore, I was trying to court my wife who was not yet my wife, which was difficult from the West Coast. Finally, I pleaded to be relieved of full-time duty on the baseball beat and recommended Terry Pluto as a replacement. I had known Terry since he was in high school at Benedictine and later when he was working his way through Cleveland State. I thought he was a natural. He was covering the Orioles for the *Baltimore Sun*. He was a hard worker. He was sober. He knew the Indians' history. He would be happy to come back home. So that's what happened.

As I turned over the beat to Terry, with a silent pledge to stay out of his way, I wrote a farewell paean to the grand old game. Years later I reflected on leaving the baseball beat and thought of the line from the Frank Sinatra song, "Regrets? I've had a few, but then again, too few to mention."

*   *   *

(*The Plain Dealer*, Dec. 25, 1979)

Yes, I'm still alive and well
Having caught a glimpse of hell.
Here's a parting, oh, so sweet
To the dreaded baseball beat.

By Dan Coughlin

Christmas came early for me this year. I celebrated it about a month ago when Terry Pluto took up residence in our sports department. He is my replacement on the baseball beat.

When he walked through the front door of *The Plain Dealer* I threw my arms around him and kissed him on both cheeks.

Goodbye baseball, hello life,
No more nightly deadline strife.
Free at last, I'm free at last,
Loose from baseball's body cast.

For the last two years, baseball has dominated my life. That may not seem like a long time to you. It is an eternity when you have been held hostage in a lockerroom.

I am like a kid turned loose in a candy store. Baseball became a gluttonous feast. Try living for two years on dessert only. You'd walk a mile for a hamburger.

Baseball is a marathon,
Endless games go on and on.
Up all night with beer and booze
Finding rhymes for win and lose.

The last two years on the baseball beat were reminiscent of my two years in the army—ours—because of the regimentation. Indians' traveling secretary Mike Seghi was the drill sergeant.

Sixteen games in fifteen days
Gives your eyes a glassy gaze.
Bus is waiting at the door;
Plane will leave at five to four.

Baseball is the most charming of games. Its pace is contemplative and relaxing. It is the only team sport not ruled by a clock. It is played to completion in two hours or four hours. Baseball never panics in the final minute.

Yet, off the field, baseball is a constant panic. There is the trading deadline. Night games have a curfew except on a team's last visit to a city. Planes have departure times which frequently are missed. Worst of all are the morning newspaper deadlines that must be met from three time zones away. It is not unknown for editors in the Eastern Time Zone to demand a story on a game that hasn't been played yet in the Pacific Time Zone.

When we play at Anaheim
At the mercy of the time
Stories come to your front door
Incomplete—no final score.

That is the most frustrating aspect of the baseball beat. Here is a game to be savored, but those of us who cover it for a living are forced to exhale stories in frantic bursts. If you're wondering how, this is how. We write stories backwards from Chicago and all other points west. The end of the story is written in the early innings, detailing how Rick Waits absorbed an early trouncing.

At the top of the story, written last, are the details of the final innings explaining how the Indians rallied to go ahead, but Victor Cruz blew up in the ninth and gave the game away.

Frustration at its extreme is when the Indians rally to tie the game in the last inning and you are rooting against them because extra innings mean you miss a deadline. The game that always was a joy eventually becomes an opponent. It is you and your deadline versus the game.

There are times on the West Coast when the papers are loaded on the trucks before the great Gary Alexander ends a game by striking out.

When you start rooting against the game you love, it's time to get out.

Find another guy to write
Passionately through the night
Observations from on high
Seen through just one jaundiced eye.

Fortunately, we have some rather understanding bosses at *The Plain Dealer*. It's not a bad place to work.

"Be a good soldier," they said. "Do a couple of years on the baseball beat and then we'll give you a reprieve. It will be good training."

This was more than reasonable. True to their word, I have received the reprieve.

Before moving along to other assignments, I was asked to write reminiscences—hopefully humorous—of my two years on the baseball beat. This is absolutely impossible.

What I remember are more than 150 lonely nights a year in hotel rooms, beginning with six uninterrupted, unpleasant weeks in Tucson, Arizona. In spring training the only respites from the boredom were nightly drinking bouts with coaches Joe Nossek and Chuck Hartenstein, trying to converse above the din of a belligerent and indefatigable combo armed to the teeth with amplifiers.

What I remember about Boston is a mouse in my room and being banned from the only all-night beanery near the hotel because of an altercation with another truculent patron. What I remember about New York is a family of cockroaches in my hotel room. And what I remember about the World Series in Baltimore was having no room at all.

So it went. If you wanted a big steak dinner, you ate at four o'clock in the afternoon because only the beaneries were open after night games in most towns. You ran the risk of developing scurvy because of a lack of fresh fruit.

Ironically, athletes on the road do not eat well, either, because conditions are the same for the entire entourage. That's why many ballplayers are in lousy shape. After games they drink all night, stumble down to the coffee shop about noon for breakfast and have a main meal of cold cuts or fried chicken while standing in their underwear in the clubhouse.

Baseball is the most glamorous of games because of the travel and media attention, but true fans are cautioned to never get too close to it.

Here's what turned my frown around:
Terry Pluto's back in town.
Now I'll live like normal men,
Free to smile and laugh again.

What Terry will find when he joins the Indians in spring train-ing is one of the nicest groups of athletes in baseball. Without a singular exception, he will find them approachable, cooperative and fun to be around.

If Mr. Pluto is a breakfast man, he can eat with manager Dave Garcia at 7:30 a.m., with Duane Kuiper, Rick Waits and Sid Monge at noon, with Rick Manning, Tony Harrah and Len Barker at 4 p.m. and with Andre Thornton all day long. For his post-game cocktail, he will have the company of half the team.

I should mention that Terry doesn't drink. Yet, I give him one year covering the Indians and he'll be a candidate for Rosary Hall, the Irish Union Club.

As for me, I'll be here writing about whatever the boss tells me to write and reading Terry Pluto's lively stories which already have caught the fancy of the readers.

Best of all, I'm going to rekindle my romance with baseball. I'll be there frequently with the rest of the fans at the Stadium—booing. I'll be there often, in fact, because I'm now a season ticket buyer.

Albert Belle: Not Easy to Like

In the winter following the 1996 season I was in the Indians' locker room for one of those typical off-season interviews with a new player. Channel 8 photographer Ted Pikturna and I finished our work. I handed him his microphone. He handed me the videotape cassette. He packed up his gear and we headed for the door. Ted couldn't get out of there fast enough. He hated baseball and he hated the pampered prima donnas who played it. I had given up arguing with him long ago. There are some good guys in the game and there are some who are hard to stomach. Albert Belle and Kenny Lofton were two of the latter.

Albert Belle was particularly unlikable. No, that's the wrong word. It's not accurate. Belle was hated. He was the most hated man in baseball. Even his teammates hated him. He once had a friend, one friend. That was Dave Nelson, the Indians' first base coach. But when Belle left the Indians and signed with the White Sox as a free agent, he broke off his friendship with Nelson and then he had no friends. That's where it stood the last I heard.

I was happy when Belle retired prematurely from the game because of a bad hip. Now I don't have to explain why I will never vote for him for the Hall of Fame. His statistics fall short. He is no longer an issue. If he had remained healthy and continued to pile up monster numbers, I would have had a problem.

"How can you not vote for him?" people would ask.

"Easy," I would say. "I knew him."

As Pikturna and I walked past, it was impossible to ignore huge cardboard boxes of mail abandoned in front of the lockers previously occupied by Belle and Lofton. These were not shoeboxes. No, these were boxes that washing machines probably came in and they were overflowing with letters and packages, all addressed to Belle and Lofton.

"What's going to happen to all this mail?" I asked a clubhouse worker.

"It will probably get thrown away," he replied.

I was aghast and agape.

"They don't want it," the clubbie explained.

There were heartfelt letters from kids that would never be opened, much less read and acknowledged.

The packages probably contained their treasures—gloves and caps and pictures—hopefully to be autographed.

Belle answered them with contempt. He ignored them.

For a player paid millions of dollars per year, it would make sense to hire a part time secretary to answer mail and send back auto-graphed pictures. Most kids would be thrilled with a form letter and a picture or a trinket.

Fans and kids, particularly kids, were of no interest to Belle. He even tried to run over a kid with his Jeep on Halloween.

To know Albert Belle is to understand Ted Pikturna.

So I thought about Lou Boudreau, the Indians' player-manager in 1948 when they won the World Series.

I was nine years old that summer and I wrote Boudreau a letter, enclosing a penny post card with Boudreau's picture. Actually, the post cards cost a nickel or a dime; the stamp was a penny. Besides the usual pictures of monuments and landmarks, many drug stores carried a line of post cards with black and white glossy photos of star Indians' players such as Boudreau, Bob Feller, Bob Lemon, Jim Hegan, Kenny Keltner and Joe Gordon.

Silly me. I actually expected Boudreau to read my letter, auto-graph the picture, lick a stamp and mail it back to me. That wouldn't take much time, but he was fairly busy. He was the shortstop and the manager and he was in the middle of a pennant race. He was also having the best year of his life and he was eventually elected the American League Most Valuable Player. Suppose a hundred kids a week wrote to him with the same request. Actually, they probably did. How stupid and inconsiderate to take up an important man's valuable time!

Three weeks later the post card came back in the mail, auto-graphed on one side and addressed to me personally in the same handwriting on the other side. It was Boudreau's handwriting, that's for sure. Everybody knew Lou's signature.

I told this story to Pikturna and he was impressed.

"That was when even baseball players had good manners," he said. "Why don't you write a column about him?"

If I had depended on Pikturna for my ideas, I would have starved to death long ago, but this time he made sense.

I called Boudreau at his home in Frankfort, Illinois, 30 miles south of Chicago's Wrigley Field where he broadcast Cubs' games for 30 years. He was retired and didn't get around very well. At the age of 79, he usually used a walker and sometimes even a wheelchair. He answered the phone on the third ring.

"Lou, what are you doing?" I asked.

"I'm sitting here in my living room going through my mail," he said. "Do you know, people still remember me? They write and ask for my autograph. Isn't that nice?"

Boudreau read off the return addresses on the envelopes, towns and cities in various parts of the country.

"Do you answer them?" I asked.

"Every one," he said.

Bob Reid Caught a Bullet

Slow pitch softball was an obsession, it was a passion, in the 1960s and '70s when hundreds of thousands of people—men and women, boys and girls—played in organized leagues in Ohio. National championship tournaments held in Cleveland and Parma attracted teams from almost every state in the union. I was often up until two o'clock in the morning covering the games. Chuck Webster, Dick Zunt, Tom Bruening and I turned softball into an important beat at *The Plain Dealer*. We thought it was important.

The very good players were often paid $50 or $100 a game. At Morgana Park in Cleveland thousands of dollars were bet on big games. It was said that more money was exchanged on some softball games than on $1,500 claiming races at Thistledown Racetrack.

Players would go off to weekend tournaments in Toledo; York, Pennsylvania, and Indiana and forget to come home.

Many teams were sponsored by bars and players were obligated to support their sponsors after games. It was really an idyllic life. You would play a game of softball and then drink beer with the boys for a few hours. It's easy to understand why the game was so popular.

I was particularly familiar with Lakewood bars. Those who played for Al Ganim's bar came home at night in sweaty uniforms that reeked of grilled onions.

Slim's Locker Room owner Bob Slimak installed shower facilities and lockers in the basement as a convenience for players who never went home.

One player who had been living in Slimak's basement did not go home for two weeks. When he eventually walked in the front door, he slid across the living room floor as though he were sliding into second base. He looked up at his wife and asked, "Safe or out?"

"Out," she said.

Slow pitch softball was a lifestyle and many wives rebelled. They grew weary of competing against softball for their husband's attention. One of them did something about it.

Bob Reid's wife hired a hit man to kill him. On the night of

Aug. 14, 1976, Reid walked through the front door of his house in Lakewood and was shot in the chest. The hit man used a shotgun loaded with a single steel ball. At close range it is good for killing buffaloes, horses and other large animals. But it didn't kill Reid.

Reid had two holes in his chest. The ball made one hole going in and after it bounced off a rib it made another hole coming back out. After all that bouncing around, the steel ball was dug out of a neighbor's roof.

This was more than an ordinary spat between an angry wife and a softball player. Reid was the best all-around softball player in Ohio and maybe the world. He could hit for power and average. He could run like an Olympic track star and he had a rocket arm, one of the best in the world.

Reid spent two weeks in the hospital and returned the next year to play at the same high level. His wife and the hit man were caught, convicted of attempted murder and went to prison. They made the mistake of leaving a witness.

When she was paroled a few years later she still had a bad attitude, so Reid didn't take any chances. He quit playing softball and moved to Florida.

Dennis Lustig: To Make a Short Story Long

Dennis Lustig always wanted to be a big man. During his reporting career at *The Plain Dealer* he interviewed some of the biggest names in sports, such as Jim Brown, Hank Aaron and Pete Rose, but he really wanted to interview Wilt Chamberlain.

Dennis stood 44 inches tall. Not even four feet. We stretched him out on the sports copy desk and measured him with a pi rule. Even other dwarfs called him Shorty. Maybe that's why he liked basketball best. He envied tall guys.

He was one of the first people Hal Lebovitz hired after becoming sports editor of *The Plain Dealer* in 1964. Dennis was 20 years old and had no newspaper experience, but he did know sports. He didn't read books, he read sports pages. He considered *Sport Magazine* highbrow literature.

Until Hal took over, executive sports editor Milt Ellis ran the sports department. Milt was a veteran. He made assignments, he designed the pages, he set policy. With Hal in charge, Milt got out of the way and watched. Hal made assignments, designed the pages and set policy. He prepared Milt for Dennis.

"I've got this fellow who's going to answer the phones," Hal told Milt. "He's kind of short."

"How short is he?" said Milt.

"He's a dwarf," said Hal.

Milt wasn't happy. Dennis started on Monday. Milt retired on Tuesday.

Dennis was hired to answer the phones in the sports department at night, giving scores and settling barroom bets. We rejoiced. It meant that we could now write our stories without interruptions from gamblers and drunks in bars.

Our euphoria, however, was shortlived—almost as short as Dennis' arms. To our horror, we discovered he couldn't reach the phones. Conditions in our work place didn't improve, they got worse.

Not only did we continue to handle the nuisance calls, but we were also fielding calls for Dennis. He gave our number to all of his Shaker Heights High School friends and half the bookies on the east side.

Nevertheless, Dennis fit in well because he was quick-witted, had a good sense of humor and happily went along with any hair-brained scheme that made him the center of attention. Dennis lived life on center stage. He was our comic relief in the office and in the bars.

When tour groups came through the newsroom, we stuffed Dennis into one of the metal coat lockers that walled off the sports department from the rest of the city room. When the visitors passed the bank of lockers, Dennis kicked and pounded on the door until one of us nonchalantly walked over and opened it. Out popped Dennis, as though nothing were unusual.

There was the election night when WEWS-TV set up the lights and camera to interview *The Plain Dealer* publisher Tom Vail live in the city room. Someone suggested to Dennis that he would soar to legendary heights if he took off his clothes and "streaked" the city room, darting between the television camera and the very proper Tom Vail, who looked almost presidential. Some of us thought that he had political ambitions and why not? Warren Harding was a newspaper publisher in Marion before he became president. James M. Cox, publisher of the *Dayton Daily News*, was a three-term governor of Ohio and the Democratic nominee for president in 1920, with Franklin D. Roosevelt as his running mate. Indifferent to such historic connections, Dennis was half-naked, down to his bare chest, when an assistant managing editor corralled him and ran him back to the sports department.

"Streaking" was a fad in the 1970s and Dennis, quintessentially trendy, ran the naked gauntlet one winter night in the Harbor Inn, a saloon in the Flats frequented at the time by longshoremen, motorcycle gangs and newspaper reporters. After neatly folding his clothes on the bar, Dennis ran the length of the bar wearing only his shoes and socks, encouraged by hoots of approval.

By then Dennis was a full-fledged card-carrying sportswriter. He couldn't answer phones, he couldn't take messages and he couldn't run for coffee so they made him a reporter. He went on the local college beat. If you were grading on a curve, he did fine.

When Ed Janka coached basketball at John Carroll University in the mid-'70s, he and Dennis became running mates. What a pair they made. Janka, a swarthy man well over six feet tall who had played basketball for Al McGuire at Marquette, was more than twice the size of the world's shortest sportswriter.

Janka met Dennis early one Saturday morning in September 1973.

"My first year at John Carroll, I was there about two months," said Janka. "I asked football coach Jerry Schweikert if I could come in and see the routine on game day. I felt some camaraderie with him. We both went to high school in Chicago. He said sure. He said he got there about 8:15 or 8:30. I went to his office and I'm leaning against the doorway. We're making small talk. Suddenly he says, 'I want you to meet our beat writer. He covers our games. Dennis Lustig.' I look around. I don't see anybody. Then I see Schweikert's eyes moving down toward the floor. I look down and there's Dennis. I felt so embarrassed. Later Dennis and I laughed about it.

"The next time I saw Dennis, he was doing previews on the local college basketball teams. He wanted to interview me. He said, 'Let's meet at the Harbor Inn.' He had to give me directions. I was sitting at the bar having a soda when he came in. He struggled to get up on the bar stool. I asked him if he needed help. He said he could make it and he did. First thing he ordered was a tall can of Foster's Lager. I thought to myself, 'I think I'm gonna like this guy.' I ordered a drink. He had another can of Foster's.

"I was uncomfortable about something, though. I was looking down at him all the time. If we were sitting in chairs we could make eye contact. I suggested that we sit at a table. He said, 'Put me on the bar.' I did. I lifted him up and put him on the bar. That worked out fine. His legs were dangling over the edge of the bar. He was actually taller than me. The preview he wrote was right on, exactly what I said.

"Dennis always was looking for a ride. He never drove. He would cover our games and I would usually drive him home. I was just glad somebody was covering our games. That's how I met his mother. We became good friends. She usually waited up for him."

Janka, who was single at the time, would sometimes bring Dennis along on dates. It was like they were double-dating except Dennis had no girl.

Dennis had all the usual sportswriter weaknesses. Drinking.

Women. Gambling. He played poker and was not good at it. He bet on baseball and was worse.

"Damn it. I bet $200 on the Indians," he said.

"An exhibition game! You bet $200 on an exhibition game?" said his pal Ken Preseren.

"I bet Gaylord Perry," said Dennis, thinking that explained everything.

Perry started and worked his three innings and left with a 3-0 lead. Five other pitchers got work and the Indians went on to lose, 16-15.

*   *   *

It was not all beer and laughter for the little guy, however.

"You should walk a day in his shoes," said his father, Leroy Lustig, who owned Lustig Advertising, a major ad agency in downtown Cleveland.

An only child, Dennis came from comfortable means. He lived with his parents in a splendid house with a heated swimming pool on South Woodland Road in Shaker Heights. Dennis' bedroom and bathroom were re-fitted with miniature accommodations, but outside the safety of home his life was strewn with terrors and difficulties. There was not one thing in life that came easy for him. It was even a struggle to get up on a barstool, even after all that practice.

He was terrified to drive. Hand controls frightened him. Often he took cabs, but he usually rode the Shaker Rapid Transit trains to work, which entailed changing to a bus at Public Square. That necessitated considerable walking on legs only 20 inches long. When he got off the bus in front of *The Plain Dealer*, he had to cross Superior Avenue, which was three lanes wide in each direction. The light always changed before he got across and he was at the mercy of drivers who could barely see the top of his head in front of their cars and trucks. He was never run over and I don't know why not.

He never had a girlfriend, but he had the same urges other guys had. He was in Cincinnati on a basketball trip with Cleveland State. He got on the hotel elevator with a tall, willowy woman who provided professional services.

"Is he a midget?" she asked Merle Levin, Cleveland State's sports information director.

"He's a dwarf," said Levin.

"I've never had a dwarf before," she said.

"Congratulations," Dennis said, looking up at her. "This is your lucky day."

Dennis rarely had a lucky day with women. They took advantage of him for free baseball tickets and used him to meet players, but Dennis had a rule. If they took the tickets, they had to take him.

Everything he did was twice as hard as for someone twice as big. One summer night he and several pals were at an Indians game at the old Stadium, lower deck behind first base, and the beers were going down smooth. Eventually nature called. But reaching the nearest men's room was like climbing Mt. Kilimanjaro for a person with legs only 20 inches long. So when everybody stood up for the seventh inning stretch, Dennis seized the moment and relieved himself on the spot.

"Who would notice?" he explained later. "There was a lot of beer spilled around there already."

After six and a half innings of drinking beer, Dennis let loose like a fire hose. Over open terrain his stream might have reached second base, except for the man in front of him who felt the backs of his legs getting wet and warm. The man turned around and was horrified to see a dwarf urinating on him. Even at a time like that, it's never good form to hit a dwarf, but there are no rules against hitting the guy standing next to the dwarf. Mayhem in Section 16 was barely averted.

In December 1967, the Browns met the Cowboys in a playoff game on Christmas Eve at the Cotton Bowl in Dallas. I spent a week in Dallas writing up the game and Dennis, desperate to be close to the action, took a week's vacation and came with me.

It was not a good trip for me, it was not a good trip for Dennis and it was not a good trip for the Browns, who got hammered, 52-14.

I turned out to be Dennis' valet. I carried his little suitcases. I unpacked them and hung up his little shirts and blazers in the closet. And when he didn't like the room I packed up everything and repeated the drill a second time. And later that night, when my snoring drove Dennis out into his own room, I packed him up a third time.

It isn't always warm in Dallas during the holidays, but that year it was unusually pleasant. One night we walked a few blocks to see the Dallas team in the American Basketball Association. On the way back, waiting to cross a downtown street, a tall Texan in cowboy boots and a ten-gallon hat looked down at Dennis and asked, "You with the circus?"

"No," Dennis said calmly, "I'm with the greatest show in football, the Cleveland Browns."

Back at the hotel, Dennis said he had to make a bathroom call. He was going to his room.

"I'm gonna get coffee and read the paper," I said. "I'll see you in the morning."

Because Dennis couldn't reach any of the elevator buttons, I walked him to the elevator and pushed his floor. I quickly stepped out before the door closed and went back to the coffee shop. I had coffee and pie and read the bulldog edition of the *Dallas Morning News* cover to cover.

Forty-five minutes later I went up to my room. When I got off the elevator and headed down the corridor, I saw Dennis standing helplessly at the door to his room. The doors did not unlock easily. It took strength and leverage to lean on the key. Dennis was reaching up, unable to turn the key with his tiny fingers. He was stranded. He could not return to the lobby to get me because he couldn't reach the button on the wall to call the elevator. If I had had another coffee, Dennis might have exploded.

Dennis had idiosyncrasies that were perfectly natural for him. He was afraid of dogs and he hated children. A dog bit him when he was a kid. What if a monstrous German shepherd looked you square in the eye and growled? Most people would be uncomfortable. Dennis was terrified. As for children, I was with Dennis at Disney World in Orlando when we were covering Miami of Ohio against Georgia in the Tangerine Bowl. Little kids came up to him and said, "Do you want to play?" That's the way kids are. Dennis reacted badly. He screamed and lunged at them, sending them scurrying in fear back to their parents.

Nobody forgot him. Over the years when I interviewed Hank Aaron and Pete Rose, they always asked, "How's Dennis?"

I loved him, but Dennis could get on people's nerves. One day Chuck Webster walked into the sports department and caught Dennis going through his mail.

"Dennis," said Webster, "I know seven dwarfs I like more than you."

I give Dennis a lot of credit. He broke his share of stories on the high school and college beats. He also developed his franchise feature, "Where Are They Now?"

In the early '70s Dennis did an innocuous little piece on one of the Indians' old players from the 1941 team and he made a passing reference to Indians' manager, "the late Roger Peckinpaugh."

The next afternoon the phone rang.

"Hey, Dennis, call for you."

"Who is it?" he said.

"The late Roger Peckinpaugh. He says he's still alive."

Peckinpaugh was 86 years old when he finally died on Nov. 17, 1977. Usually when a notable personage died, someone from the death notice department hand-carried a carbon copy to the news room, which was the case with Peckinpaugh.

"A guy named Peckinpaugh died. Supposedly he managed the Indians. Anybody here interested?" said the person who took the information.

Dennis looked up from his typewriter and said triumphantly, "I had that five years ago."

Dennis knew when his own time would come. Doctors told him his type of dwarfism came with a 40-year life span. His tired heart stopped on schedule on November 25, 1984. He left small shoes to fill—size 4½. Every year on the anniversary of his death some of his old chums leave a six-pack of Bud Light on his grave—five empties and one unopened.

Hal Lebovitz:
"Too Highly Principled"

Hal Lebovitz was the smartest man I ever knew. He was the most fair, the most loyal and the most influential. He shared his experiences with me in bits and pieces over 18 years. I learned a lot just by paying attention.

He graduated from Glenville High School at the age of 16 and went on to Western Reserve University, where he majored in chemistry and played football and basketball. At about 6 feet, 3 inches tall he was considered a big man. Today he'd be a point guard. After graduation he taught chemistry at Euclid Central High School and coached the baseball team. He collaborated with another teacher to write a chemistry textbook that schools used for decades.

While in high school he had a summer job with the Cleveland Recreation Department as a playground instructor on the near west side, where a bully was tormenting younger and smaller children. There was only one way to bring him into line.

"I had to fight him," said Hal, who normally was not belligerent. Hal won and the bully troubled no one after that.

While coaching baseball at Euclid Central in the late 1930s he began feeding news and notes about high school baseball to the *Cleveland News*. He promoted not only his own team, he promoted every team. The *News* had a four-man sports staff—even in those days it was a skeleton staff—and they were grateful for the well-written stories. This led to a full-time job at the *News* in 1942. Hal loved teaching and coaching but there was no teachers' union in those days. There was a newspaper union, however, and the newspaper job tripled his salary.

In the summers of his youth he umpired sandlot baseball. He talked about working on Sundays for a quarter a game from morning until the sun went down. He rode streetcars from ballfield to ballfield, lugging his mask, shin guards and chest protector with him. He umpired up to five games on a typical Sunday. It was the Depression and every quarter helped.

He also officiated high school and college football and basketball. Abe Saperstein once asked him to be the permanent referee for the Harlem Globetrotters. The job paid a nice salary but the globe trotting part was the hang up.

Hal spoke wistfully of many happy Saturday afternoons officiating small college football in the Ohio Conference. He and his wife, Marge, would pack a lunch and stop for a picnic along the way to Muskingum or Tiffin. There was a time, in the 1920s and '30s, when sportswriters commonly had side jobs refereeing big time college football. Knute Rockne of Notre Dame often hired his sports writing pals, which fueled his publicity machine and certainly did not hurt his won-lost record. According to historian Murray Sperber, Rockne's files contain correspondence from sportswriters begging for these plum assignments and promising good work, whatever that meant.

Hal seemed to particularly enjoy officiating high school football. He was the referee for the 1950 Charity Game at the Stadium, which was postponed for two weeks because of the colossal Thanksgiving weekend blizzard. Hal woke up on that Saturday morning to find two feet of snow on the ground. Nothing moved. The roads were impassable.

Hal walked from his house on Edgerton Road. in University Heights to Cedar Road, where a bus somehow was plodding through the snow. Hal rode the bus to Public Square and walked down West 3rd Street to the Stadium and discovered he was the only one there. The game was postponed not for a day or a week, but for two weeks until Saturday, Dec. 9. Hal walked back up the hill to Superior Avenue and walked to the *News* building at East 18th Street and Superior and helped put out the Saturday afternoon paper, which was never delivered due to the storm.

He remained active as a football official into the 1970s. After rules interpretation meetings the officials frequently adjourned to Hal's house in University Heights to discuss nuances and knotty problems.

"Ask Hal, the Referee," wasn't merely a clever logo for his question and answer column, Hal the Referee was his alter ego.

*   *   *

During the entire 1950s Hal was the traveling baseball writer for the *News*, which featured the most exciting sports pages in town. I know. I delivered the *News*.

What impressed me most about Hal as a baseball writer was his strict adherence to kosher dietary rules. He never strayed, which meant that he usually went to bed hungry after getting out of the ballpark at midnight, too late to find a kosher meal or even a snack in most American League towns. Years later, when I traveled the baseball beat, I realized what a hardship this was on him. Even at sports banquets when a separate fish dinner wasn't prepared for Hal, he would simply decline the meal without complaint and eat an extra salad.

Hal was on the beat in 1958 when the Indians experienced their fourth straight year of declining attendance and William R. Daley, president and largest stockholder, was discouraged. The Indians were losing money and Daley, 66, a self-made millionaire and generous philanthropist, was a stranger to red ink. He called the board of directors together and asserted that Cleveland would no longer support Major League baseball. He wanted to move the team to Minneapolis. Several of the nine members of the board of directors were in favor of the move.

Hal told me that he called several members of the board and threatened to expose their treachery and cause them endless torment, pointing out that their family names would be stained for generations. Most were long-time Clevelanders. Daley, for example, was originally from Ashtabula but became a towering figure in Cleveland's Catholic community. He was president of Catholic Charities and served on the University of Notre Dame's advisory council. He donated $100,000 to Marymount College in New York. With Hal's threats ringing in their ears, the directors relented and they were rewarded. The Indians rebounded in 1959. They were in the pennant race until the middle of September and more than doubled their home attendance.

When the *Cleveland Press* bought the *News* and shut it down on Jan. 20, 1960, Hal was out of work for exactly 24 hours. Gordon Cobbledick, sports editor of *The Plain Dealer,* hired him immediately as the sports feature writer.

Cobbledick retired in 1964 and Hal was promoted to sports

editor, using his pulpit to continue saving the Indians. Attendance had plummeted for four straight years again. Innuendoes and veiled threats resurfaced that they were on the move. Hal used his sports pages to support a "Save the Indians" game in 1965, proving that baseball still had a pulse in Cleveland.

Over subsequent years under Hal, *The Plain Dealer* sponsored Bat Day, Ball Day and Cap Day, leading to every other kind of baseball giveaway you can think of. Left to their own devices, in the 1970s the Indians promoted a deodorant giveaway on Mother's Day.

*   *   *

Hal made other contributions to sports in Cleveland. For instance, when big time pro soccer was introduced to Cleveland in 1967, Hal supported it without reservation, even though he was never interested in the game. He appointed me the pro soccer writer and sent me to England for two weeks to learn the game.

"While you're there, see if there's an auto race you can cover," Hal said.

So I spent two weeks with the Stoke City team, a major league pro team in England. In those days it was called First Division. Today it is called the Premier Division. In 1967 Stoke City played its summer schedule at the Stadium, representing Cleveland in the new United Soccer League.

All this came about because the 1966 World Cup final was shown on live television by Public Broadcasting at 10 o'clock on a Saturday morning in this country and it actually registered a blip on the ratings meter.

When promoters saw that, two professional leagues were formed overnight and Vernon Stouffer bought a franchise for Cleveland. Stouffer owned the Indians at the time and Gabe Paul, president of the team, advised Stouffer that they would be wise to control the summer competition for the entertainment dollar.

In their haste to get the league in motion for the 1967 season, entire teams were imported from overseas and Canada to represent American cities. Cleveland drew Stoke City, England.

"Get a passport and pack your bags," said Hal.

"Yes, sir," I said.

And as for finding an auto race to cover, the Grand Prix of Monaco at Monte Carlo conveniently followed my two-week sojourn to England. The night before the race I was drinking French beer at the bar of the Hotel d' Paris on the square in Monte Carlo when I noticed that every pair of eyes was looking in the same direction. I followed them to a small cocktail table in the middle of the lounge 30 feet from me. Sitting there were race car driver Graham Hill, who finished second the next day, with two friends from London, Richard Burton and Elizabeth Taylor. This was in 1967. She and I were both in our primes.

Chuck Webster, the lawyer, was a sportswriter at *The Plain Dealer* in those days and he said to me more than once, "You get trips like that all the time. You must have incriminating pictures of Hal or Tom Vail. Perhaps with farm animals. Do you?"

Those were the glory days of newspapering. *The Plain Dealer* presses rolled out more than 400,000 papers a day, thick with advertising. They could have been printing dollar bills. My job was to help them spend it.

Pro soccer was a flop. It lasted two years and then quietly went away. Stouffer lost a million dollars with it in 1967. He sold the franchise to Ted Bonda and future U.S. Senator Howard Metzenbaum in 1968 and they lost another million. Nobody cared. Attendance fluctuated at around 5,000 per game. Nevertheless, Hal sent me flying all over the country with them for two straight summers and he told me why.

"I don't want anybody to say pro soccer failed because *The Plain Dealer* didn't support it. They can never blame us," Hal said.

There was a reason Hal felt strongly about this. Cleveland was an original member of the NBA in the 1946-47 season but owner Al Sutphin, who also owned the Barons hockey team and the Cleveland Arena on Euclid Avenue, turned the franchise back to the league after only one year because the newspapers did not support it. At *The Plain Dealer*, Gordon Cobbledick was disinterested. At *The Cleveland Press,* sports editor and columnist Franklin (Whitey) Lewis was openly hostile to pro basketball. Sutphin felt betrayed and rightfully so.

Hal was a pro basketball fan. He felt the media in Cleveland misused its power of life and death and he vowed he would never commit the same crime. Cleveland waited 24 years for its second chance with pro basketball.

During Ted Stepien's brief regime as owner of the Cavs, the eccentric Stepien had to be handled with kid gloves. Those were difficult days for the entire NBA and the league's biggest problem was in Cleveland, where Stepien blindly destroyed the franchise with ridiculous trades and stupid draft choices. NBA commissioner Larry O'Brien usually began each day with a call to Lebovitz, asking, "What is he doing now?" Hal was the Henry Kissinger of the NBA. He advised the commissioner on how to handle the Stepien crisis. They came up with a plan to prohibit the Cavs from trading draft choices. Eventually, when Stepien sold to brothers George and Gordon Gund, included in the deal was a unique arrangement allowing the Cavs to buy extra draft choices from the league to replace the ones Stepien had foolishly traded away.

*   *   *

Hal turned his back on baseball only once. The All-Star Game was scheduled for Cleveland in 1981, the year the season was interrupted by a two-month strike. When the strike was settled, the season was resumed with the All-Star Game on Aug. 9 and 72,086 baseball hungry fans turned out on a Sunday night, the all-time largest crowd for an All-Star Game.

Hal, however, felt the players should have played their way into shape with a few games before the All-Star Game. He wrote that Cleveland was getting tainted All-Stars.

American League public relations director Bob Holbrook was sent to Cleveland a few days before the game to appease Hal. I greeted Holbrook and two assistants from the league office in the lobby of *The Plain Dealer* and led them to Hal's office and left them alone. They talked for 30 minutes. Afterward I led them back to the lobby.

"Hal is highly principled," I said as we walked toward the elevator.

"He's too highly principled," Holbrook said.

Not even Hal was perfect.

The Mysterious E. J. Kissell

When the old *Plain Dealer* police reporter E.J. Kissell died a few years ago at the age of 68, I went to his funeral service out of curiosity. Hardly anyone really knew E.J. His life was a mystery. No one even knew his home phone number, not even the city desk.

A life-long bachelor, E.J. worked the night shift. He usually was on duty until about 3 a.m., when the last paper rolled off the presses. For many of those years he worked out of the press room at the old Central Police Station in downtown Cleveland. Because some people never saw him, they wondered if E.J. Kissell really existed or if the byline was some rewrite man's non de plume or a code known only to the city desk.

"If he had two friends, he made sure they never met," said an old acquaintance.

It turns out that he had more than two friends. He had many and they were unmasked at his service at St. Peter's Catholic Church across the street from *The Plain Dealer* building on Superior Avenue. Several people bounded up to the microphone to talk about him and everyone, it seemed, knew a different E.J. Kissell.

Dick Peery, a veteran reporter who rubbed shoulders with Kissell at Central Police Station in the 1970s, said, "The first two years I knew him I thought he was a detective."

They worked for the same newspaper.

"I would see him on Thursday mornings when he came in for his check," said Dick Zunt, the old sportswriter. "He was a historian. He was an expert on the old Cleveland Barons hockey team and the Cleveland Buckeyes of the Negro National League."

"He played hockey," somebody else said. "He played in an amateur league for many years. I saw him sneaking out one night with his skates. He tried to hide them behind his back."

"He liked old movies, family-type stuff," said Jerry Kvet, a police reporter for the rival *Cleveland Press*. "Every Sunday he would come to my house with a movie projector, screen and reel of film. He would show old Blondie and Dagwood movies. I thought he probably did this with other people until one time he asked if he could just leave the projector in my living room. After watching Blondie and Dagwood about eight times, I asked him if he could bring a different movie."

About 40 old reporters and deskmen attended the service. I suspected most were like me. They were curious about this enigmatic man who was known only by his byline.

One person was different, however. A lady who said she had been Kissell's special friend for more than 30 years told gentle stories about his kindness.

"But I always wondered," she said, "if someday I would discover that he had a wife and three kids in Garfield Heights."

Newspapermen have a well-known fascination for eccentric people. Sometimes you find them very close to home.

Pete Gaughan:
Human Can Opener

When the doctor advised Pete Gaughan to quit drinking, Pete's first question was, "For how long?"

"For forever," said the doctor.

"Forever!" said Pete. "That will kill me."

"Then either way, you're gonna die," said the sawbones. "If you keep drinking, your gall bladder will have to come out, you'll get kidney stones and then your other organs will fail. You'll never see 60."

Pete drank Grey Goose vodka. He drank it like Dennis McLain drank Pepsi Cola. Dennis McLain, you'll recall, consumed 24 bottles of Pepsi a day in 1968 when he won 31 games for the Tigers. In other words, Pete drank a lot of Grey Goose.

But he agreed to give abstinence his best shot. Thinking they were helpful, his friends said, "Try pot, try pills." But Pete ignored them.

"It worked out," he said after the first year. "I feel better in the morning. I no longer have hangovers and I have money in my pocket. I'm saving up for a hip replacement."

It was the spring of 2010 and Pete was limping badly, which made it difficult in his line of work. He was a 57-year-old caddy at Canterbury Golf Club in Beachwood. He smiled at the symmetry of his life. His first job as a kid in the 1960s was caddying at Canterbury and he will probably go out the same way, carrying doubles on a Sunday in 90-degree heat.

In the middle of his life he was a radio announcer, newspaper sportswriter, high school football referee, gambler, bookmaker, drinker and performer.

Mostly, for 25 years he was a sportswriter for the *Sun Papers*, a chain of weeklies that served the Cleveland suburbs. He worked for a weekly but he had a cult following that no daily newspaper star ever enjoyed.

Pete led a charmed life, the Hollywood stereotype of the untamed newspaperman. But Pete was real. He was unlike any other person, living or dead, real or imagined. Some people suspected that Pete was crazy. Others knew he was.

For example, when he was at Ashland University, majoring in radio and television, he was known as Crazy Pete because at the start of every varsity basketball game he swung down on a rope from a door near the ceiling of Kates Gymnasium to the basketball court like a circus acrobat. His jumping off point was an architectural aberration, a door near the ceiling that opened into a straight 35-foot drop to the gym floor. Why a door opened to nothingness, only the architect knew. Maybe they ran out of money and never added the stairs. In the long history of the field house, Pete Gaughan was the only one who ever used the door.

The first time Crazy Pete did it, his parents were at the game and they were shocked. They left at halftime.

"Here," his father said, throwing a Superman tee shirt at him. "Your mother's in the car crying. Good bye."

Pete added sunglasses, a used overcoat and a hat from a re-sale shop to the Superman tee shirt and he became a star. The PA announcer always gave Crazy Pete a big buildup and for two years he was an institution. One night the Ashland team refused to take the floor until Pete had performed. The acclaim increased Pete's appetite for the spotlight. Years later he was asked to reprise the stunt. He did, but the rope was different. It was slippery, and Pete lost his grip. He plummeted 35 feet to mid-court, almost killing himself.

Upon graduation in 1975, Pete was tipped off to a job by his classmate, John Telich, who later wound up in television at WJW Channel 8 in Cleveland. They were the broadcast team for Ashland football and Bucyrus High School football. Telich landed his first television job in South Dakota, Pete went to work as a country disc jockey on WBCO in Bucyrus, Ohio, where he read the farm reports in between tunes.

"Here we are with the hog scores," Pete would say.

"Don't call them hog scores," the general manager said.

"Why not?" Pete said impudently. "WBCO stands for wheat, beans, corn and oats."

Pete made quite an impression. They planned to fire him after only one week.

"That first weekend they gave me a list of commercials to make. It was a real load. Nobody could have made them all and that would have been an excuse to fire me. But I had nothing else to do so I worked all weekend and made them all. I was good at making commercials. I stayed two years there and got into sports," he said.

In 1978 the Bucyrus *Telegraph-Forum* ran a help-wanted ad for an assistant sports editor and Pete got the job.

"I wasn't trained for newspapers," Pete recalled. "My first game story was like a radio script—I typed it all in capital letters and spelled it 'last nite.'"

Sports editor Rusty Miller confronted him.

"I thought we had editors to catch things like that," said Pete.

"You are the editor," said Miller.

They didn't allow things such as spelling, syntax and style get in the way of a beautiful friendship. Rusty Miller and Pete were the same age. They soon shared an apartment. They were colleagues and drinking buddies. Rusty taught Pete to love Ohio State football. Rusty went on to become Ohio sports editor for the Associated Press, one of the most important men in Ohio journalism.

"He taught me to get your work done, then party. I liked to do it at the same time," said Pete. "We made sports writing fun. We were out in the community. We were known for reporter involvement. I learned to take pictures and develop the film. One time I forgot to put film in the camera. Everyone saw me taking pictures and the next day we ran an announcement, 'Due to technical difficulties, we do not have pictures of the Bucyrus High School game.' I was making a hundred bucks a week and I felt like a millionaire.

"That's where I bit off the top of a beer can for the first time. We were watching the 'Incredible Hulk' on television and I said, 'If you guys piss me off, I'm biting the top of this beer can off and turning into the Incredible Hulk.' So I did. I got my mouth around the top of the can and punched a hole in it with a tooth and I spun the can around like a can opener. Off came the top. I chugged the beer and then I held up the top of the can and said, 'I love these easy opening tops.' Naturally, I cut my mouth and was bleeding profusely. It's not a party unless somebody's bleeding. A legend was born."

And here, dear readers, we have arrived at the essence of Pete Gaughan, blood gushing from his mouth and thousands cheering for him. In a previous life he would have starred in a Roman colosseum. This is the reason Pete Gaughan never was invited to speak at a high school career day.

He eventually brought his show home. After four years in Bucyrus, he came home to Cleveland in 1980 and landed a job on the copy desk of Sun Newspapers, with the promise that he would get the first opening in sports. True to their word, he soon was covering sports in the eastern suburbs.

In 1984 he made his first appearance in *The Plain Dealer*.

On opening day of the baseball season he and some friends sneaked cans of beer into the old Stadium. Pete had decided to turn pro. When Indians' rookie Otis Nixon came to bat, Pete jumped on top of the Indians' dugout with a sign that said simply, "Otis." When Nixon tripled, Pete unfurled the rest of the sign that said, "My Man," a nod to the classic line in the movie, *Animal House*. The fans went crazy. Then Pete pulled out a can of Miller Lite, put it to his mouth, ripped the top off and chugged the beer. The fans responded as though the Indians had just won the pennant. In the Indians' dugout players looked around, they looked at each other, they poked their heads over the top of the dugout in disbelief.

"It was magical," Pete recalled.

Jim Neff, a general columnist for *The Plain Dealer*, was in the press box and was paying attention. He rushed down to interview Pete.

"Not now," said Pete, half-drunk and bleeding all over himself.

They talked a few days later, however, and Neff wrote a nice piece about him.

The following year on opening day *The Plain Dealer* was prepared. A photographer caught a beautiful picture of Pete ripping the top off another beer can and Pete wound up on page one. His fame was spreading.

"Jerry Gordon, the general manager of Sun Newspapers, called me in the next Monday. He had some concerns about me being on page one, but he didn't mind a free spirit. I always appreciated him letting me do it," said Pete.

Each March he covered the state basketball finals but he never saw a game. For 20 years he spent three days and nights in the Varsity Club, the bar near Ohio State's St. John Arena where the high school tournament games were played. The crowd, back to back and belly to belly, cheered for Pete to chomp off the tops of beer cans and he went through them like a metallic Pac Man.

"I'd come back from Columbus every year and it looked like I was in a knife fight," he said.

One guy wanted a private performance.

"I did it for him. I charged him $100," said Pete.

Like an old west gunfighter, Pete was sometimes challenged to defend his reputation.

"A guy came in the Varsity Club and demanded a challenge match. Naturally, I accepted. The crowd counted down, hundreds of people, 'Ten. Nine. Eight . . .' I rip my can open and chug my beer and he's still trying to get the top off. 'He's an amateur. Throw this man out,' I shouted and two bouncers grabbed him and threw him out.

"The next year this same guy comes up to me in the Varsity Club and he says, 'Do you remember me?' He unbuttoned his shirt and showed me his tee shirt. It said, 'I love these easy to open tops.' He said he wanted to challenge me again. He had gotten pretty good. I bet he practiced for an entire year. Our cans hit the floor at the same time. It was a tie. I said, 'To be the champ, you've got to beat the champ.' The bouncers threw him out."

Drunk or sober, bleeding or not, Pete was easy to recognize because of his unique dress code. He always wore pajama pants and Hawaiian shirts, regardless of the weather or the season. Anybody could drink beer, bleed on himself and write about sports. Pete wanted to stand out from the crowd. He wanted to look distinctive.

And that's how he did it for almost 25 years at Sun Newspapers. He was a fixture at high school football and basketball games. When he wasn't covering them, he was betting on them. And when he wasn't betting on them, he booked the bets.

Pete was proud of what he did.

"We were a community paper and we covered our communities. Being a weekly, I didn't have to go back to the paper and write. When Joe Lynch was coaching Chanel, I would interview him by the light of the jukebox at the Golden Coin. We were a fraternity. I made friends for life. Joe Lynch. Jim Cappelletti. Sean O'Toole."

Pete also appreciated the Crunch indoor soccer team. The Crunch is out of business now but it enjoyed a unique status in the 1990s. It was the only Cleveland team since the 1964 Browns to win a league championship.

"In 1994 the Crunch was playing for the championship downtown at the Cleveland State Convocation Center. I said we had to be there. The first championship in 30 years. I got four other guys to come with me. I had to drag two of them kicking and screaming. They weren't into it yet," he said.

"I wanted to look particularly good so I wore my stars and stripes pants, Hawaiian shirt and my pink tuxedo jacket with the sleeves cut off," he said.

On their way downtown they stopped in a bar to put on their game faces and they had glorious snootfuls by the time they arrived at the Convocation Center.

The Crunch trailed the St. Louis Ambush, 15-10, late in the fourth quarter but rallied to tie the game, 15-15, and went into sudden death overtime.

Crunch goalie Otto Orf was spectacular in the 15-minute sudden death period. St. Louis outshot the Crunch, 15-1, but Orf turned back every shot and the game remained tied. They went to a second sudden death overtime and Hector Marinaro's goal in the early minutes won it for the Crunch.

The Convocation Center exploded. On the carpet at midfield it looked like a jailbreak with Crunch players running around like lunatics. Pete rose to the occasion with one of his greatest performances.

"This is better than 1964. I've got to be part of this," he said, rushing down from the media section to the playing field.

"Hector was holding the trophy in the air over his head and I ran up to him and helped him hold the trophy. I had one hand on the trophy when three cops made a beeline for me. They grabbed me. I said, 'I'm the media,' and I showed them my credential. They took my credential and threw me out."

Pete recalled driving one of his friends home to Cleveland Heights and then returning downtown to join the celebration at Shooter's, where everybody was buying drinks. From there he caught up with the Crunch team party at Fanatics, a bar near East 9th Street, where they drank until 4:30 in the morning.

"Everything he says is true," said Chuck Murr, who was the Crunch publicity man at the time, "except he didn't tell you the part about going to jail that night. He wrote about that in his column."

If he phoned in his column from jail it gives new meaning to the term "cell phone."

He got into golf in 1980 and before long was betting hundreds of dollars a round.

"I could play with anybody. Give me two shots a hole and I can beat Tiger," he said.

By the mid-'90s he was in a group of about 10 high rollers who played every Tuesday, Wednesday and Thursday for thousands of dollars.

"Andy Cannavino said we're living like millionaires three days a week," Pete recalled. "One day it rained so we played putt-putt indoors. I lost $3,000 in one match of putt-putt when a guy hit a hole in one off a rock. But I had seven grand in my pocket from booking."

Pete was married once. The ceremony was at St. Ann's Church in Cleveland Heights. Among the guests were John and Jane Telich.

"When we entered the church, Pete's brother, Hank, the usher, asked us, smoking or non-smoking?" said John.

The marriage lasted four months. They split up but soon reconciled and that didn't work either.

"I said I was going out for milk. I came home a week later. I said all the stores were out of milk. I could never adjust to going home at night," Pete said.

I think you've got to be a sportswriter to understand Pete Gaughan. Obviously, his wife didn't and we can sympathize with her. Pete's father, a fireman and a high school football referee, didn't understand him either.

"What kind of job is this where you sleep till noon?" he once asked his son.

Pete followed in his father's footsteps as a referee because he took a course in football officiating when he was a freshman at Ashland.

"I got an A in it, thank God," said Pete, "because I was on probation and I needed the grade."

They worked a high school varsity game together for the first time in 1980. Chances are, Pete had a bet on it.

In 2005 Pete quit Sun Newspapers after a quarter of a century and moved to Phoenix to work for a start-up golf publication, that failed within two years. He moved back and picked up the bags at Canterbury. Sun Newspapers were no longer hiring.

Pete, you didn't miss a thing. But we missed a lot.

Joe Tait: "He Came With the Franchise"

When he bought the Cavs, Dan Gilbert came in with a big broom and he used it. I'll never forget the change of command press conference when somebody lobbed the traditional question at Gordon Gund, who had just sold the team to Gilbert.

"What advice would you give the new owner?" somebody asked.

"Patience," said Gund. "He should be patient."

That, I thought, is the last thing the inert franchise needed. The Cavs required dynamics and, thankfully, Gilbert knew that. He was a man of action.

Radio broadcaster Joe Tait had no idea where he stood. Gilbert quickly fired coach Paul Silas. He did not retain television broadcaster Michael Reghi. Tait suspected he also had a bulls' eye on his chest. When Gilbert introduced the legendary radio announcer to Mrs. Gilbert, he said, "This is Joe Tait. He came with the franchise." That was all. No enthusiasm. No elaboration. Not even a job description. He could have been introducing the oldest elevator operator in the building.

Whatever happened, Tait was prepared to take it like a man. He was, after all, past retirement age. And don't forget, he almost didn't take the job in the first place back in October, 1970. But Gilbert chose not to disturb the legend, for which a multitude of Cavs' fans are grateful.

In all of broadcasting, Tait is unique. He remains the only major league play-by-play man to work his games solo. He has no sidekick, no color analyst, no stats man. He keeps his own running box score. So let's turn back the clock and relive a moment in time during the 1976 playoff series with the Washington Bullets. This column ran in *The Plain Dealer* on April 27, 1976:

> Landover, Md.—We sat around the lunch table, which is what traveling sportswriters do before they sit down for dinner, and

prodded the story of the Cavaliers' genesis from two men who were there in the beginning, Bill Nichols and Joe Tait.

When Nichols was handed the job of pro basketball writer for *The Plain Dealer*, nobody lined up to offer congratulations. I didn't know whether to send flowers or a Mass card.

"That first year nobody second-guessed what I wrote," Nichols recalled, "because nobody read it."

Tait confessed that he almost quit 12 hours after accepting the job as radio voice of the basketball team.

Actually, Tait wasn't aboard for the team's maiden voyage. He was hired several games into the first season in October of 1970. Bob Brown, assistant to Cavs' founder Nick Mileti, broadcast the first several games while Mileti pondered which route to take.

"He didn't know whether to go to New York and get a big time broadcaster, or bring one in from the sticks," Tait said as he chewed on a char-broiled cheeseburger. "After a few games Nick knew it would be disastrous to hire a big timer. The team was so bad the guy probably would quit after three weeks or he'd knock the team so bad they would have wished he would quit."

Cavs' coach Bill Fitch told Mileti he knew a sportscaster in Terre Haute, Ind., who was so dumb he probably would take the job. Mileti couldn't believe anybody was that dumb and he wanted to meet him.

"I had given up sportscasting by then," Tait said. "I was the general manager of a station in Terre Haute. I wasn't going to beat the bushes all my life and wind up a broken down sportscaster in a small town at the age of 50.

"I had known Bill Fitch when he was coaching Coe College and I was broadcasting at Monmouth College. We had the worst team in the conference. When he got the Cleveland job, I wrote him a letter of congratulations. My application for the broadcasting job was a P.S. at the end of the letter. 'Do you want me to do the same thing for you that I did at Monmouth College?' I said.

"When Bill talked to me he warned me that the Cavaliers were a bad team. 'As bad as Monmouth?' I said. 'Worse,' he said."

So Tait came to Cleveland to meet Mileti, who told him to broadcast a game into a tape recorder. That night Mileti listened to the tape and the next morning at 9 a.m. he called him and offered him the job. As dumb as Tait was, he even made the Cavaliers sound exciting. Mileti liked that. So did thousands of listeners, it turned out.

"I went home to Terre Haute that night to pack my bags and I listened to Andy Musser broadcast the 76ers-Cavs game from Philadelphia. I almost backed out of the deal that night," said Tait.

That was the game the Cavaliers, who were still winless, lost by 54 points. Afterward, Fitch fined every player $54.

During his broadcast, Musser seemed in awe of the Cavs' ineptitude.

"This team is so bad it won't win a game this season," Musser said. "The Cavaliers aren't good enough to play in the Eastern League. It's the worst team I've ever seen. When the Cleveland fans see how bad they are, they won't come to the games and the team will go broke. I don't know how they'll last the season. This might be the only time we'll ever see this team."

Tait said he was serious. He almost called the whole thing off.

"But Nick figured I'd be impressed by the big city, the tall buildings, the airplanes and the hotels—and he was right," said Tait.

I met Tait for the first time several games later in San Francisco, where that night the Cavs lost their 15th straight game, setting the NBA record for ineptitude. Late in the game during a time out, Bingo Smith urged his teammates to rally. "Let's go. We're only down by 10," said Smith. Fitch looked up at the scoreboard which said Warriors 96, Cavaliers 66, and he knew math was not Smith's forte.

That was the night a security guard refused to let Fitch in the auditorium because he didn't have a ticket. The guard relented because he said nobody would admit to being the coach of the Cavaliers unless he really was.

That night Fitch, Tait and I walked back to the hotel through a wet San Francisco fog and Fitch stopped to berate a fire hydrant. Fitch was seething. "Johnny Egan couldn't guard that fireplug," he said.

The next night in Portland the Cavs won their first game by one point, but they weren't sure the game was over because the buzzer failed to work. Tait had to ask into a live microphone,

"Did we win?" It was the first of only 15 games the Cavs won that first season of 1970-71.

A few weeks later the Cavs beat Philadelphia and Andy Musser, who was in Minneapolis on a football assignment, spilled a beer all over himself when he saw the score on television.

The next year when Stretch Howard refused to tape a halftime interview with Tait, Rick Roberson grabbed him and ordered him to do the interview. "He's the only one who says anything nice about us," said Roberson.

Those were the things we talked about while awaiting the showdown Monday night with the Washington Bullets. We had to keep reminding ourselves that yesterday's nightmare and today's dream world are all part of the same story.

Bob Buck: A Tragic End

American sports fans have thrilled to the voices of some outstanding sports announcing families. For example, there were three generations of the Caray family—Harry Caray, Skip Caray and Chip Caray—all baseball announcers. There are the Albert brothers—Marv Albert, Al Albert and Steve Albert.

Most people are familiar with the father-son tandem of Jack Buck and Joe Buck in St. Louis, but do you remember the third member of that golden-voiced family? Sadly, not many do. Jack Buck's youngest brother, Bob Buck, who would be the uncle of Joe Buck, currently the number one sportscaster on the Fox network, flirted with stardom but kept slipping on banana peels.

Bob was a network quality broadcaster, also, and I'm not saying that just because he and I were boyhood chums from Blossom Park Avenue in Lakewood, Ohio. I heard Bob broadcast University of Michigan football games on the radio. I heard him do a Rose Bowl game on NBC radio. He did weekend sports on ABC radio. He was the sports director of KMOX-TV in St. Louis. These are just a few of his jobs from a long list. Bob moved around a lot and I know why. His bosses were psychopaths, every last one of them, out of their minds, one crazier than the next. I never knew anyone so unlucky.

This is Bob's story. If there are any exaggerations, and there probably are, they are his alone. Bob could tell a good story and I was a good listener. So keep in mind, this story is essentially true except for the parts that might not be.

Let's go back to his first job after graduating from Lakewood High School in 1956. He joined the Army and they shipped him to a 65-man transportation unit in France.

"My first sergeant was an idiot," Bob confided to me. "He would not let me try out for the division baseball team."

While Bob was slaving in the kitchen one morning—perspiring, dirty and covered with grease—he spotted the general touring the installation. Without bothering to salute, Bob approached the general and informed him of the first sergeant's antagonism toward baseball. Bob wound up on the baseball team, but he also took up permanent residence in the first sergeant's doghouse. "When the baseball season ends, your ass belongs to me," the first sergeant told Bob.

Bob's ass always seemed to be in trouble.

The war was over and there was no fighting in France, but Bob changed all that. While on a baseball trip to Berlin, Bob triggered a beer garden brawl between his team and a group of Soviet soldiers. Maybe that's why they built the Berlin Wall three years later. Maybe it also was the reason Bob never made corporal.

Back at his installation in France, Bob was the permanent one-man detail to raise the flag at 5:30 every morning.

"Because we were in France, we were required to raise the French flag first so it would fly above the American flag," Bob recalled. "One morning I cut holes in the French flag so I could fly it backwards. There were about 300 French paratroopers stationed down the road from us. Every morning they'd run in formation past our barracks. When they came running past that morning, they went crazy. They came over the fence and kicked our asses from barracks to motor pool and back. I was lucky I didn't wind up in the stockade."

As usual, Bob absorbed the brunt of the consequences while the first sergeant, who could not control his own troops, skated free. That's the military, for you.

After his discharge, France's gain was Cleveland's loss. Bob came home and took a job with the Cleveland Transit System. Once, while driving a Rapid Transit train, he opened the doors on the wrong side of the car and dumped a passenger onto the adjacent track.

"He had a tough time climbing back in," said Bob. "At first all I saw were his fingers and his hands. I stayed in my bulletproof cage and talked to him over the microphone."

While driving Rapid Transit trains Bob introduced racing to the rails. He and another driver would talk to each other on pay phones from opposite ends of the line. When they hung up, they would run to their trains and the race was on.

"We would fly through stations at full speed. No stopping. The wind almost blew people off the platforms. When we got to the other end, we would run to the phone. If it was already ringing, you lost," Bob said with delight.

His superiors were not delighted. They transferred him to buses.

"Late one night in a blizzard I was the only bus at Public Square. There were people scattered all around the Square waiting for their buses. Instead of letting them stand out there and freeze, I kept driving around picking them up so they could wait in my bus. An inspector came up and told me to wait in my regular spot. I told him where to go. I picked up my change box and quit. When I got off the bus, everybody applauded. But I had to walk all the way home to Lakewood."

Next came a job as a bank teller at the Cleveland Trust branch at West 117th Street and Detroit Avenue. It lasted only three weeks.

"When we got our first shipments of Kennedy half dollars the manager told us not to give them to anybody unless they had $65,000 in their savings account. Late that afternoon a little old lady came in. Every week she took a bus to the bank to deposit one dollar. She asked me if we had any Kennedy half dollars. 'Sure,' I said. 'Here's two of them.' The branch manager was standing behind me. He started bellowing, berating me in front of everybody, so I picked up my money box and threw it all over the bank. Then I got my coat and walked out."

He also worked on the Lakewood Fire Department, he was a typist for *The Plain Dealer* and he clerked on the railroad. The Buck family had a long railroad history. The Erie Railroad transferred his father to Cleveland from Holyoke, Massachusetts, in 1939, when Bob was one year old.

In 1966, with his brother Jack a star in St. Louis, Bob succumbed to the lure of broadcasting. I wasn't surprised. It was in his blood. When we were kids Bob and I ran string about 100 feet across the street from his bedroom window to mine and attached the ends to empty cans of Campbell's tomato soup. After dinner we would give each other the baseball scores. "Get on your can," we would call across the street to each other. This went on until the neighbors complained that our sagging string became tangled on their cars, especially in the rain.

When we played one-on-one baseball with a tennis ball against the back wall of Franklin Elementary School in Lakewood, Bob announced the games as we were playing. He always was the Red Sox. When he was pitching he was Mel Parnell and when he was batting he was Ted Williams. I was the Indians and when I batted, I was Lou Boudreau. In real life, Boudreau had great success against

Parnell, but behind Franklin Elementary Boudreau never got a hit off Parnell.

"Strike three. Down goes Boudreau," Bob would announce with authority and finality, the concise style of the era. Then he would chuckle. I hated that.

Bob turned pro in 1966 on Lakewood's fledgling cable TV outlet. He moved on to radio and television stations in Mansfield and Peoria before landing in St. Louis in 1971. With his older brother's help Bob was hired as sports director at KMOX-TV, one of the most prestigious jobs in broadcasting.

In St. Louis the Buck name had cachet. Jack was the voice of the Cardinals on KMOX radio and Bob was the perfect complement on television. He was smooth. He was younger. He looked good. He sounded great.

KMOX-TV also carried the football Cardinals exhibition games and Bob was the play-by-play man with a great deal of latitude. The problem was, Bob had more attitude than latitude. Most broadcast teams are composed of a professional TV guy and an ex-player. Bob picked his own analyst and he chose a local bartender named John McMann. As the story goes, McMann was hilarious. Bob discovered him pouring drinks in a saloon and said, "I'm going to make you famous." McMann was pleased. "This one's on me," he said.

McMann had personality. The fans loved him for his candor and his turn of a phrase. The *Washington Post* even did a story on him. The St. Louis papers lavished him with praise and that's when the trouble began. One of the papers discovered that besides announcing football and pouring drinks, McMann held down a third job. He was the city dogcatcher, a full-time job, his primary job, the job that provided his pension and benefits, and the job to which McMann devoted only two hours a day. He would catch the occasional stray and then report for duty in the saloon. When people complained that St. Louis was going to the dogs, they could point to McMann. Fame turned on him like an ungrateful cur. His popularity waned in the face of a snarling populace. The city let him go and so did KMOX-TV, which was embarrassed by the publicity.

Bob, however, kept his promise to McMann. He made him famous.

When KMOX-TV fired Bob in September 1975, the dogcatcher had nothing to do with it. Bob managed that all by himself.

"The reason they gave for firing me was that I was unsatisfactory," Bob told me at the time. "But the real reason was that I delivered a commentary critical of the CBS network special, 'The Guns of Autumn.' I don't like to shoot animals, but I thought the program was grossly unfair to hunters. It painted them as killers and madmen and 98 percent of them aren't that. It was biased, slanted and unobjective reporting. Journalism is supposed to present the facts.

"When I handed my script to the news director, he ordered me not to use my commentary. The producer cautioned me not to use it. They didn't come right out and say I'd be fired, but they said I'd be looking for trouble if I didn't substitute another commentary."

As I said earlier, Bob's bosses always seemed to be off their meds. They needed therapy. He was so unlucky.

Bob stuck to his guns and squeezed off a stinging attack. Taking shots at CBS was doubly unwise because KMOX was not merely an affiliate of CBS, it was owned by CBS. The network was overwhelmed with complaints about the anti-hunting special. Criticism from the National Rifle Association was expected and CBS had no choice but to shut up and take it, but getting ambushed by its own employee was unforgivable. Bob was fired seven days later.

Bob believed his defense of hunters was a morality test because he himself was not a hunter. He did not believe in shooting animals, but he defended the right of others to shoot them. He believed that he was defending the Constitution of the United States.

While Bob himself never shot an animal, he had no problem shooting humans. Hell, he shot me!

When we were in grade school, Bob and I regularly engaged in BB gun fights at Andrews Field in Lakewood. In the winter we would crawl through the snow firing off shots at each other from 40 or 50 yards away. We were bundled up and couldn't feel it if we were hit, unless we took a shot in the face or the eye, which never happened. It did happen to the great Browns and Red Sox announcer Ken Coleman, however. Not many people knew that he was blind in one eye. A friend shot him in the eye with a BB gun when he was a kid.

Anyway, back to Bob and his itchy trigger finger. At St. Clement grade school, we always came home for lunch. It was a short walk and we had a 75-minute lunch break. Bob called me on the phone and said, "Come on over, I have something to show you."

I ran across the street and rushed in his side door. I closed the door behind me and turned to go up three steps to the kitchen when I heard the familiar "Snap" of a BB gun and my rear end caught fire. Bob was standing at the bottom of the basement stairs and he had just shot me in the ass. It throbbed the rest of the afternoon and I had to sit on it in class.

Bushwhacked by my own guy. I could sympathize with CBS.

After getting canned in St. Louis, Bob was a fill-in radio play-by-play man for the San Antonio Spurs of the American Basketball Association. It was only temporary and it didn't pay much. After one season, Bob and his wife, Martha, and their daughter, Colleen, came home to Cleveland to regroup. They were staying with Martha's parents, who had a small, yappy dog. I stopped by to loan Bob a few hundred dollars. Times were tough between jobs. I reached down to pet the dog and he leaped up at my face and bit the hell out of my nose. Blood was gushing from the wound. There was much shouting and running around for Band-Aids and hydrogen peroxide. When they got done with me I looked like Jack Nicholson in the movie, *Chinatown.*

Bob seemed to ride through life on a pogo stick. He bounced up and down over the later years. One year he was a newsman on Cleveland radio station WGAR. Another year he did University of Michigan football on WWJ in Detroit, where NBC radio heard him and whisked him off to New York as its network weekend sports announcer. When he was up he did well. We were together in Lake Placid covering the 1980 Winter Olympics. He was with NBC, I was with *The Plain Dealer.*

In 1981 he called me.

"I'd like to congratulate myself for one of the smartest moves of my professional career," he said, his voice dripping with sarcasm.

A year earlier Buck left his $55,000 a year job with NBC for a higher-paying job with Enterprise Radio, an ambitious new sports network in Hartford, Conn. Within a year it went bust.

Bob was temporarily beaten down.

"I've had it with this business," he said in a rare moment of despair.

He wanted me to place an ad for him in *The Plain Dealer.* He was serious, so I placed the ad. It said he was looking for a career change to a more stable field. He got calls from real estate people.

Luckily, he stumbled into a radio job in Evansville, Ind., as the voice of the Evansville Aces college basketball and baseball teams and host of a call-in radio show. Things seemed to be looking up but not really.

In 1990, after years of excruciating back pain, his wife, Martha, gave up the fight and took her own life. It was not an easy life. Bob dragged her and their daughter, Colleen, back and forth across the country for over 20 years. Periodically, they were forced to retreat back home and stay with relatives until the next opportunity opened up. Bob's brothers and sisters wanted to wring his neck many times.

Sometimes, however, even a guy with a black cloud over his head gets an even break. Bob met his second wife in Evansville. Not only was she beautiful, but she was supportive and encouraging. She even seemed to enjoy his stories, though I'm not sure why. I'm also not sure that she knew what she signed up for. He and Carole were married in Evansville in the early 1990s. The sun shone brilliantly on them and for the first time in years his days seemed to be joyous from beginning to end. I was happy for him.

The last time I saw Bob alive was in the summer of 1995 when he and Carole paid a visit. They sat in our sunroom and Bob talked about his plans to write a book about his life. He never finished it. On Jan. 22, 1996, Bob chose to end it all. He went down in the basement and put a plastic bag over his head. He couldn't get off that pogo stick.

Dudley and Neal:
Enemies to the End

Owners of radio station WERE believed the stars were aligned when they matched Jimmy Dudley and Bob Neal as their baseball announcing tandem in 1957. Dudley already was a star. He had been the Indians' lead announcer since 1948 and was hugely popular. Neal also had impressive credentials. He had been the Browns' first football radio play-by-play man and had done baseball on the Mutual Radio Network. This could have been the best announcing team in baseball history. But alas, this blending of two great talents turned into a collision of two monster egos.

"He thought he should be number one and I knew I was number one," Dudley said when I visited him in Tucson in February, 1979.

Dudley was 39 years old when he landed in Cleveland in 1948, just in time to ride the wave of the great Indian uprising. Dudley had bounced around radio for almost two decades, announcing minor league baseball in the South and Cubs games in Chicago. But in Cleveland he hit the jackpot. Within a year of sliding into the broadcast booth next to his partner, Jack Graney, Dudley owned the town.

He probably would have sounded more natural doing the Chattanooga Lookouts games in the Southern Association, but his folksy banter and down home expressions caught the fancy of Cleveland baseball fans. "The string is out" was a full count on the batter and a hitter on a streak was "hotter than a two-dollar pistol." And instead of goodbye, it was "lots of good luck, ya hcah."

Yes, he was in the right place at the right time. Cleveland went baseball crazy in 1948 as the Indians won the pennant and the World Series. It was Cleveland's first world championship in 28 years. It seemed like a long time back then.

Dudley claimed that his broadcasts captivated black audiences in cities across the Indians' radio network because in 1947 they became the first team in the American League to break the color barrier with Larry Doby, who was the starting centerfielder. In mid-season of 1948 the Indians added relief pitcher Satchel Paige, the 42-year-old star of the Negro National League.

The Indians set an attendance record of 2.6 million paid admissions in 1948. Those who were not at the games were never far from a radio. You could walk down any street in Northeastern Ohio on a summer day or evening and never miss a pitch. In those days before air conditioning, Dudley's voice crackled from every open window and from front porches where families gathered to listen. Men sat on folding chairs in their driveways and drank Erin Brew, which for many years was the main sponsor of Indians games.

When the 1949 season began I sent in my 50 cents for Jimmy Dudley's official Indians press guide and scorebook. I must have been away at college or in the Army when it got tossed out with some of my other cherished childhood treasures, such as Lou Boudreau's autographed photograph.

In the early 1950s, when Dudley also announced the Browns games on television for a couple of years and had his daily radio show on WERE, the only Cleveland radio personality who could match his income was legendary disc jockey Bill Randle. Dudley averaged $90,000 a year, more than any Cleveland athlete except Bob Feller. He made three times as much as Otto Graham. He made more than Paul Brown. The buying power of Dudley's income would be like $1 million today. No Cleveland media personality comes close to that today. Nobody even makes half of that.

Dudley announced Indians games for 12 happy years and eight others when his partner was Bob Neal, an exquisite announcer with a commanding presence. Neal had done Browns football on the radio from 1946-51 and handled with aplomb the Mutual Radio Network's baseball game of the day, All-Star Games and World Series games. Neal was smooth. He was network smooth.

There was a mystique about them, enhanced by their unique relationship. They hated each other. The only thing holding them together was enmity. They wouldn't talk to each other on the air or off.

At one time the Indians' flagship station, WERE, insisted that they sign an amicus clause in their contracts—an agreement to get along.

"The truce lasted about one week," said Dick Miller, whose family owned the station.

When Dudley was hospitalized after a serious heart attack on the final day of the 1963 season in Kansas City, someone asked Neal if he would visit him. Dudley was in intensive care.

"Yeah," Neal replied, "I'm going to pull the plug."

They were teamed up for only eight seasons between 1957 and 1967, but it seemed like a lifetime to those caught in the crossfire. There was a three-year break in the middle when they were separated—one on the radio, the other on television—like boxers sent to neutral corners after a knockdown.

I never knew why they clashed. They never could explain it. It was easier to understand those ethnic feuds that churn for centuries in Europe and Asia. They each had a streak of vanity, but that's not uncommon in that business. In fact, vanity might have been the only thing they had in common. They both wanted to be number one.

"They could have worked side-by-side on an assembly line in a factory and they still wouldn't get along. They were just two different personalities," said Dick Satterwaite, the radio engineer for Browns and Indians broadcasts for decades.

Neal complained that when he was on the air "doing his innings," Dudley would rifle gnawed chicken bones into an empty metal wastebasket in their tiny broadcast booth. Maybe it happened once but Neal told the story a thousand times.

"It made a hell of a racket and he did it on purpose," Neal would roar.

Actually, they were rarely in the booth at the same time. When one was on the air, the other would socialize with the newspapermen on the other side of the press box where the writers worked.

One problem was that Dudley was the "lead" announcer, he had seniority, having joined the Indians' broadcast team in 1948. Neal was already in Cleveland, but he was calling Browns football games. Dudley was slightly older, born in 1909. Neal was seven years his junior, but no one dared tell Neal he was junior to anyone.

They came from different cultures. Dudley was born in Alexandria, Virginia, and went on to earn a chemistry degree from the University of Virginia. He was not a big man physically, but he was a decent high school athlete, playing football, basketball and baseball. He lost his hair as a teenager. He was bald as a cue ball.

"The result of a stupid prank," he told me once. "For high school graduation, six of us shaved our heads. I used a razor. Down to my scalp. Smooth as a baby's behind. Then I went to Virginia Beach to work as a lifeguard that summer. I got such a bad sunburn on my head that my hair never grew back. I've been bald since I was 18."

As a result, Dudley was rarely seen without a hat.

"The Stetson hat company starting sending me hats," Dudley told me. "I had dozens of them."

Dudley was proud of his southern accent, at a time when some of baseball's most popular announcers were southerners, such as Red Barber, Mel Allen, Lindsey Nelson, Herb Carneal and Ernie Harwell.

"Our accents appealed to people," he once said. "They were sort of graceful. They fit in with the game. Dixie speaking is slow, leisurely, and baseball is that kind of game."

On the other hand, Neal was "urbane," the word used to describe him by *The Plain Dealer* sports editor Hal Lebovitz.

Neal came from a totally different culture. He even had a different name. He was christened Norman Lilli in 1916 at his Catholic baptism in Canada, but he changed it to something more sporty. Son of a mining engineer, he rebelled at entering the mines and left home when he was 17. His years between 1933 and 1943 are vague. He thought of becoming a doctor but did not study medicine.

In Detroit he ran into singer Johnny Desmond, who influenced him. He studied music at Julliard School in New York City and was a trained opera singer. When World War II broke out he joined the U.S. Army Air Corps. Like most Canadians, Neal grew up with a hockey mentality but his range of expertise was vast. He was a competent hockey announcer and an outstanding football play-by-play man. He came to Cleveland in 1944 and joined WGAR as an announcer. He was the Browns' first radio announcer from 1946 to 1951, when Bill McColgan succeeded him.

"Neal had a good relationship with Paul Brown," the engineer Satterwaite recalled. "On Friday nights Paul Brown had Bob over to his house to go over the playbook."

Neal was a big-time play-by-play announcer on the Mutual Radio Network in the mid-1950s. In 1954 and '55 he broadcast the baseball game of the day. He also did baseball All-Star Games and the World

Series in 1955 and '56. He called Ohio State and Baltimore Colts football on radio.

"But I could never do the Indians and Browns on radio in the same year because of the beer sponsors," Neal once told me.

Erin Brew sponsored Indians games, Carling was the Browns sponsor, and the announcers were closely identified with the products because many of the commercials were done live between innings. By 1957 his Browns days were over and Neal joined the Indians radio team. Despite his national reputation, he was second banana to Dudley in the broadcast booth.

Dudley was chatty and had an easy manner. Fans would yell at him from passing cars as he walked jauntily down the street and he waved back as though he knew them. The fans liked him and he knew it. It made him confident.

"He was a schmoozer," recalled Dino Lucarelli, an Indians PR man of that era.

Neal was a hard-edged businessman. He became a director of Park View Federal Savings and Loan and was part owner of radio station WNCO in Ashland.

"Both were extremely talented," said Satterwaite. "Dudley was more friendly, extroverted. Bob Neal was more intelligent."

Neal also was aloof, not easily approachable, occasionally abrasive and regal. He did not seem to have many friends, but I liked him. Not many people did.

"He has the aloof manner of a seminarian bucking for bishop," wrote James B. Flanagan in a *Plain Dealer Sunday Magazine* article in 1968.

The tension in the broadcast booth was so intense that by the late 1960s it was clear that somebody had to go. In December 1967, I interviewed Dudley for a story in *The Plain Dealer Sunday Magazine*, for which I would have earned an extra $150. He was secure and comfortable.

"They can never fire me," he told me. "My fans would never allow it."

But before I could write the magazine piece, Indians president Gabe Paul and WERE general manager Harry Dennis dropped the hammer. On Friday, Jan. 19, 1968, they fired Dudley.

"I consider it a kick in the teeth and a lousy thing to happen after all the years I have been with the Indians," he raged.

The next day I took my magazine notes and wrote a straight story for the Sunday sports section. There went Dudley. There went $150 . . .

Sunday, Jan. 21, 1968
The Plain Dealer

Exactly a month ago Jimmy Dudley reflected on his 20 years with the Cleveland Indians. He was proud of his career here. It all began, you know, with the Indians' world championship season of 1948.

"I've been through 10 managers, five ownerships, two stations and dozens of sponsors," he recollected.

And, he might have added, he outlasted five different broadcasting partners until he was fired Friday as the Indians' radio play-by-play voice.

How secure Jimmy felt one month ago. People had tried to fire him in the past. His middle South approach to broadcasting rankled some critics. He had always weathered the storms. But he did offer a note of caution.

"In radio and TV you never can feel too secure," he said. How prophetic he was. "But if it were left up to a vote of the fans," he added, "I think I'd be pretty secure."

Innocently enough, Jimmy pegged an underlying reason why he is no longer the Indians' baseball announcer. He was talking about his relationship with Bob Neal, his broadcasting partner, and their inability to develop a warm camaraderie.

"We don't have the repartee announcers in other cities have," he admitted. "I don't understand it. I wish I knew why. The first part of every season we're going great guns with great repartee. Then, it disintegrates. I guess we fail to give our listeners what we could."

A month ago Jimmy talked of retirement "in five or six years." Retirement had nothing to do with the heart attack he suffered in spring training a few seasons back. He said he was completely recovered. He quit smoking and limited his drinking.

Jack Graney was Dudley's favorite partner. "He taught me a good deal of humility," Dudley says. "He had a great philosophy. 'Remember that 95 percent of the people who listen to you know more baseball than you think they do.' Graney went on the theory that he was the eyes of the people who weren't at the ball games."

Later, Dudley teamed with Ed Edwards for one season, Tom Manning for two, Bob Neal, Harry Jones and then Neal again.

Jimmy has made a considerable amount of money broadcasting baseball. "Baseball is a moneymaker," he admitted. "You can do baseball alone with nothing else and make good money. You do 162 games. Television, for instance, carries only about 60 games."

If Jimmy doesn't latch onto another broadcasting job, he can retire next to the 10th green at the Tucson Country Club, where his winter home lies. He has an 11 handicap. He shoots in the low eighties.

"I've always wanted to do an article about the most unforgettable person I've ever met," Jimmy said once. "I'd like to write a story about Satchel Paige."

Jimmy may have the time to do it now.

Years later Jimmy reflected on his glorious era with the Indians.

"Nobody was more of a homer than I was," he admitted. "I loved the Indians. They were my life. I hated the Yankees as much as any fan. But you don't have to be a stooge. Broadcasters are the eyes of the baseball fan. You paint the word picture. The greatest letter I ever received was from a blind boy in Toronto. He closed saying, 'Goodbye, Jimmy. Remember, you are my eyes.'"

Gabe Paul did not completely abandon Jimmy. Gabe helped him get the broadcasting job with the expansion Seattle Pilots in 1969, but after only one season the Pilots moved to Milwaukee and became the Brewers. They did not take Dudley with them. Dudley soon retired to Tucson, where Jimmy and his wife, Angie, enjoyed many happy and peaceful years in the home they bought in 1963.

In the meantime, his commercials continued to run on Cleveland television until his death. Most people born after 1960 don't remember Dudley as a baseball announcer, they know him as the television pitchman for the Aluminum Siding Corporation of America and the phone number that became ingrained on our consciousness— Garfield 1-2323.

"He gave our company a face. He gave us legitimacy," Herb Schoen, president of the company, said when Jimmy died.

Dudley was 89 when he died on Feb. 12, 1999, of Alzheimer's.

*   *   *

Sadly, Neal's final years were emotionally and physically tormented. In 1966, when he was 50, he and his wife, Virginia, divorced, and from that point his life became a soap opera. We talked about that when I visited him at his home in California shortly before his death.

"My romantic tragedies, they were tragedies for the women in my life," he said. "It wasn't my fault. It was one of those age things. I didn't want to be an old man. Virginia got a big settlement. She deserved it."

A few years later he met Diane K. McCormick, a secretary who worked at WERE, and he fell head over heels. Some people cynically call it the "Silly Old Fool Syndrome." Neal called it love. In 1971 he proposed to Diane, who was less than half his age. She said, "Yes." Then she exercised a woman's prerogative.

She changed her mind.

Suddenly their little winter-spring romance became page one news. Neal actually filed a breach of promise lawsuit in Cuyahoga County Common Pleas Court. Who in the name of heaven actually does that when a courtship ends?

In the evening of March 8, 1972, Bob and I flew home together from Sarasota, Florida, where we had covered a special meeting of the American League owners to consider Nick Mileti's bid to buy the Indians from Vernon Stouffer. The other owners were not comfortable with Mileti's financing plan. Although his second presentation later that month was accepted, that night he was denied. There was a lot of rejection going around.

We changed planes in Atlanta. Our plane was one of the last ones out. It was well into the evening and we had to wait in the airport lounge, much to the chagrin of the bartender who wanted to close and go home. Bob and I sat at one end of the bar. Mileti and his PR man, Bob Brown, brooded and paced nervously at the other end of the bar. I don't know who was more unhappy, Mileti for being voted down by the owners or Neal, who was voted down by his true love. The night was starting to get weird.

Bob and I talked quietly. He had one drink. I had one beer. We were both stone sober. Suddenly Bob reached into his pocket for his wallet and pulled out a photograph of the lovely Miss McCormick, the object of his affection and the object of his lawsuit. He grew emotional. He professed his love and I think there was a tear in his eye. I was very uncomfortable. Here was a majestic man, almost 56 years old, pouring out his heart to a 33-year-old sports-writer.

"She's beautiful, isn't she?" he said.

Of course she was. She was ravishing. I reassured him that she was movie star lovely.

"I love her," he said.

I knew he did. Anyone who would make a page one fool of himself had to be in love.

However, only days later both Neal and Mileti brightened. The American League owners met again and changed their minds. They ratified his new financial plan. Mileti and his partners became the new owners of the Indians.

The very lovely Miss McCormick also changed her mind. She gave Bob Neal thumbs up and he put a ring on her finger in April 1972. He was 56. She was 25.

Bob's attitude changed. He was euphoric. He would frequently wander over to the writers' half of the press box with binoculars slung around his neck to search her out. It was usually Sunday after-noons and she was invariably in the centerfield bleaches drinking beer and sunning herself. He would hand me the binoculars.

"Look at all those empty beer cups," Bob would marvel.

For Diane, life was a party and she was at the epicenter of it. But the party ended in tragedy. They were married for only three months.

On Sunday, July 9, 1972, after a doubleheader at the Stadium, Bob arrived home to their penthouse apartment in the Carlyle, a high rise on Lakewood's Gold Coast. He greeted Diane and retreated to the room he converted to an office to write his script for the next morning's sports report on WERE. As he typed, his life changed forever.

"This is the story he told me," said Satterwaite. "He was in his office writing his script. He heard a commotion. He went out on the balcony and saw Diane lying on the restaurant roof below them. She was standing on a folding chair watering some hanging plants. She fell over the railing."

She plunged 200 feet and landed on the roof of the Silver Quill Restaurant, which was connected to the high rise. Her service at Brown-Forward Funeral Home on Chagrin Blvd. in Shaker Heights was by invitation only. Satterwaite and his wife were there. So were Jim Schraitle and his wife. Jim was another engineer. Herb Score also was invited.

There was a small procession to Calvary Cemetery and that was it. A short, joyous period of Bob Neal's life was over.

There were whispered suspicions that she didn't fall, she was pushed, but I never bought that theory. Dick Satterwaite didn't, either.

"He was genuinely broken up," said Satterwaite. "After he came back, somebody said something. He broke into tears. You know, what people try to say but they're awkward about it."

"I was crushed," he said to me during our last visit in 1979. "It wasn't a sex thing. She bubbled. She lit up a room."

When the 1972 season ended, Mileti totally restructured the Indians' radio operation. He moved their games from 5,000-watt WERE (1300) to WWWE (1100), the 50,000-watt station recently purchased by Mileti's investment group. He also changed lead announcers. He fired Neal and replaced him with Joe Tait, the Cavs basketball announcer, who did double duty on basketball and baseball.

"What an ingrate," said Neal. "I introduced Mileti to all the people he should know and this is how he says thanks."

Neal's health spiraled downward. His kidney disease worsened. It was first diagnosed in 1942, which led to his discharge from the U.S. Army Air Corps. By 1974 his kidneys were permanently out of business. While being treated for kidney failure in 1974, they detected and patched an aneurism on his aorta just in time. He began kidney dialysis every other day. A bovine vein was implanted in his left forearm as a permanent port for the dialysis. He became weak. He suffered two heart attacks and underwent a triple bypass.

"When I had the triple bypass, it was one time in my life I wasn't frightened," he said. "I came to realize if this is my time, I'm ready. I called on my latent faith. 'Lord, I've been an in and out type guy. I haven't always been the nicest guy in the world.' I had absolutely no fear."

His body was a disaster, but he refused to wave the white flag.

"When I went into kidney failure, a doctor advised me to die with dignity. He gave me a book to read, *Above the Clouds*, or something. He advised me this was the way to go. He said he would never go through the torment of a kidney machine, the needle going into you every other day. He described it as 'being on the cross.' Sure it hurts, both going in and coming out, but every day I get is a bonus. I can play golf. I can play with the neighborhood kids. It's better than being dead," he said.

Neal was not quite dead. He still had one more romance, this time with Robin Gardiner, the leasing agent for his downtown apartment building, the Park Centre. Neal was sick and alone. She offered to do his shopping. Soon she was driving him to his kidney dialysis sessions at the Cleveland Clinic.

"She was doing so much for me that I asked her how much she made as a leasing agent. I told her if she could manage the dialysis technique, I'll hire you as a nurse-secretary. She took home study courses in running the dialysis machine."

They were married in 1975 and moved to LaCosta, Calif., north of San Diego, where they had a nice house on a hill overlooking a golf course. One room was converted into a hospital room where she plugged him into the dialysis machine every other day.

"Some guy said I should do radio commentaries here in San Diego," he said. "I don't think they could take it. If you want to see a community that has subjugated truth for endearment, this is it—the land of fruits and nuts. The attitude toward their teams is, 'Don't knock 'em. They might move.' They fought so hard for a major league baseball franchise. The rap against some broadcasters is that they shill. I've heard them all. They all shill."

He couldn't help it. He was bitter to the end. And that's where it ended in 1983 when his heart gave out. Bob was only 67. Jimmy Dudley did not attend Bob's funeral. Dudley was the last man standing. He was number one again.

1. That's my dad in the three-piece suit and me at the age of seven entering the stadium for the 1945 charity game between Cathedral Latin and St. Ignatius. *(Cathedral Latin Yearbook, 1946, courtesy of the alumni association)*

2. I came out from deep cover after posing as Hubert Hopeful, a new member of the Parma High School football team in 1967, while writing a series of articles for the *Plain Dealer*. I was more than a decade older than my teammates. *(Plain Dealer)*

3. At my desk at the *Plain Dealer*. Back then, a newspaper was an insane asylum with no locks on the doors. Any registered eccentric could sashay through the front door, ride the elevator to the second floor and parade through the city room. Crazy was normal in those days. Now, nobody gets inside without a printed invitation and a security clearance. Characters are not welcome. *(Mike Edwards)*

4. Olympic athlete Stella Walsh would often breeze into the *Plain Dealer* sports department unannounced to promote one of the girls sports teams she coached. She would always challenge me to a running race. *What kind of a cad would humiliate an old lady in a hundred-yard dash?* I thought. But I raced her anyway. She ran me into the ground at Cuyahoga Heights High School track and then drank me under the table at an East Side tavern. *(Cleveland State University Special Collections-Cleveland Press Archives)*

5. In 1967, the *Plain Dealer* selected Collinwood football coach Joe Trivisonno in a Favorite Coach contest that was part of our circulation battle with the *Press*. We sent Trivisonno and his wife to Pasadena to watch the Rose Bowl . . . on television. *(Plain Dealer)*

6. Rocky Colavito enjoyed a long love affair with the fans and a long disdain for former Indians general manager Frank Lane. *(Cleveland State University Special Collections-Cleveland Press Archives)*

7. Indians shortstop Lou Boudreau was pure class, on and off the field. He still answered fan mail, years after retiring. Then there was Albert Belle, who treated fans with contempt and left boxes full of fan mail unopened. *(Cleveland State University Special Collections-Cleveland Press Archives)*

8. Bob Feller negotiating his 1948 contract with Indians owner Bill Veeck. It contained an attendance bonus of a nickel a head every time he pitched at home. The Indians drew a record 2.6 million people. *(Cleveland State University Special Collections-Cleveland Press Archives)*

9. When there was a big announcement in the Cleveland sports world you would usually see us all together: (l to r) Hal Lebovitz, me, Chuck Heaton and Russ Schneider. *(Bill Wynne)*

10. Indians announcers Jimmy Dudley (left) and Bob Neal were never really this close. They hated each other. They never spoke to each other on or off the air. *(Cleveland State University Special Collections-Cleveland Press Archives)*

11. "He came with the franchise," Dan Gilbert said of Joe Tait when Gilbert bought the Cavaliers in 2002. Tait first took the Cavs job back in 1970. Young and clean-shaven back then, Joe didn't know any better. *(Cleveland State University Special Collections-Cleveland Press Archives)*

12. Inch-for-inch, Dennis Lustig was the most outrageous person I ever worked with. He happily went along with any hare-brained scheme that made him the center of attention. He also interviewed some of the biggest names in sports. Here we are at a party at Chester Commons in downtown Cleveland, 1974. (*Author's Collection*)

13. Paul Brown celebrates the 1949 All-American Conference championship with (clockwise, starting in upper-lefthand corner) George Young (52), Lou Groza, Warren Lahr, Lou Saban (20) and Edgar "Special Delivery" Jones. (*Cleveland State University Special Collections-Cleveland Press Archives*)

14. Despite progressing deafness, Browns coach Blanton Collier led the team to the 1964 championship. Here he is flanked by quarterback Frank Ryan (l) and halfback Jim Brown. Paul Brown apparently never forgave him for taking over after Brown was fired. (*Cleveland State University Special Collections-Cleveland Press Archives*)

15. Art Modell was saying goodbye long before he sold the Browns. He gave hints, but nobody listened. Modell's Browns had plenty of problems, but the expansion Browns that replaced them were a fiasco in every aspect. *(Cleveland State University Special Collections-Cleveland Press Archives)*

16. Ohio State coach Woody Hayes was a great recruiter. He was a great orator, too, but when he tried to persuade campus antiwar protestors, they didn't listen. *(Cleveland State University Special Collections-Cleveland Press Archives)*

17. Legendary Browns tackle Doug Dieken was flagged for a mile of holding penalties in his 14-year career. He held everything that moved. *(Mike Edwards)*

18. Mario Andretti took his life in his hands riding with me in the Indianapolis Speedway. Standing are (l) Parnelli Jones and Lloyd Ruby. *(Author's Collection)*

19. Junior O'Malley died a thousand deaths at the racetrack. He proved the old adage, "All horse players die broke." At Thistledown one time he marked all 10 races and didn't pick a single winner. "Do you realize how hard that is?" he said. *(Cleveland State University Special Collections-Cleveland Press Archives)*

20. Barry Clemens, called one of the greatest shooters of all time, played on some really bad teams before he got to Cleveland. *(Cleveland State University Special Collections- Cleveland Press Archives)*

21. Hal Lebovitz was the smartest man I ever knew. And versatile: He taught chemistry, wrote a textbook, coached high school baseball, umpired and was even asked to be the permanent referee for the Harlem Globetrotters. He also kept the Indians from being moved out of Cleveland. Twice. *(Courtesy of Neil Lebovitz)*

22. Muhammad Ali and Jim Brown, two of the greatest living athletes, together in Cleveland. I interviewed Ali in 1964 at the Majestic Hotel on East 55th Street. It was just the two of us (no handlers back then). He was surprisingly candid—and a living contradiction. *(Cleveland State University Special Collections-Cleveland Press Archives)*

23. Boxing promoter Don Elbaum (l) with two of his best fighters, Tap Harris (center) and Doyle Baird. Both were dangerous in and out of the ring. *(Cleveland State University Special Collections-Cleveland Press Archives)*

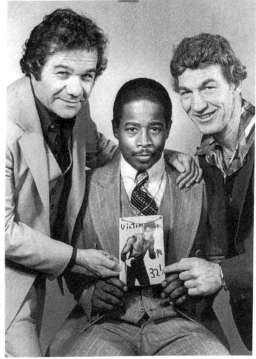

24. In the 1950s, soccer was played in Cleveland mostly by ethnic groups—some with historic rivalries that inspired crowds to violence. When the *Plain Dealer* ran my story about Lucky Kramer, word got around that *this* referee was carrying more than a whistle—he also had a .38 snub-nose in his waistband. He got a little more respect. *(June Kramer)*

25. A *Plain Dealer* photographer went looking for Pete Gaughan on Opening Day in 1985, hoping he'd repeat his stunt from the previous year: biting off the top of his beer can. Gaughan did not disappoint, and this photo ran on Page One. *(Plain Dealer)*

26. Secretariat (left) and Dan Coughlin (with all his fingers). *(Author's Collection)*

27. I worked the fun years at WJW-TV newsroom. From left: Dick Goddard, Ralph Tarsitano, me and Tim Taylor, 2003. *(Author's Collection)*

28. Shooting behind the scenes of our Friday night show. (l to r) Dan Jovic, John Telich, me and Tony Rizzo. *(Andy Fishman)*

Blanton Collier:
He Couldn't Hear the Cheers

He was football's Beethoven—a genius who overcame deafness to reach the top of his game.

Blanton Collier coached the Browns to the NFL championship in 1964 and to the NFL championship game three other times in his nine years as head coach, a remarkable achievement for anyone, much less someone with such a severe handicap. He never complained. He had dealt with it all his life. His environment was a world of jumbled words, static and strange sounds. The media never trumpeted his disability. It would have been disrespectful and impolite to publicly trespass on his privacy.

In 1982, a year before he died, Blanton and I sat at his kitchen table in a development outside Houston. I sat facing him so he could read my lips. He recalled growing up in Paris, Kentucky, which is near Lexington.

"I thought I was socially backward. Nobody ever talked to me," he said. "I would sit in the waiting room of the doctor's office. I noticed everyone talking to each other but never to me. They probably said something to me, but unless I was looking directly at them, I didn't know it. I could not hear them."

They may have thought the young lad was disinterested or even rude, which could not have been farther from the truth. He was well-mannered and considerate, all the days of his life.

Despite the handicap, he became a teacher and coach at his alma mater, Paris High School. He was head coach of all the boys teams—football, basketball, baseball and track. His specialty was basketball. After all, in Kentucky, basketball always was king. His boys teams won four state championships. One winter the girls basketball coach took ill so he also coached the girls team. He also became a swimming instructor. Probably because of his hearing disability, he relied on his eyes, not only to read lips, but in every pursuit. As a coach he studied motion, footwork, leverage. He became a great teacher because he was a great student.

When the United States entered World War II, Collier was 35 years old. He was married and had children. He was a high school teacher, an acclaimed coach, and he was deaf. Few men in America were less eligible to be drafted but few were more eager to go. He had his master's degree in educational administration and he was working on his doctorate. He had outgrown Paris, Kentucky.

"If there wasn't a drastic change in my life, I would always be just a high school coach," he told me that night at his kitchen table. "I thought if I joined the service it would force me to make a big move."

He signed up for the army.

"They turned me down," he said. "I couldn't pass the hearing test."

The navy was a different story, however. He learned how they gave the test, he learned how to beat it and he passed. He got measured for his bell-bottom trousers. He was headed for a date with destiny.

At Great Lakes Naval Training Station in Chicago, the navy discovered he couldn't hear, so what could they do with him? He had been hanging out at the base football practices, where Paul Brown was coaching. Brown's reputation was well-known, having coached at Ohio State. They became acquainted and Brown was dazzled. He discovered that this unknown enlisted man knew his football, so Collier was re-assigned as an assistant coach, the only enlisted man on a staff of officers. Brown began to rely on him.

Collier returned to Kentucky when the war ended in 1945. He rejoined his family and waited for the phone to ring. When it did, Paul Brown was on the other end of the line. He was putting the original Cleveland Browns together and he wanted Collier to be his top assistant coach, his right-hand man.

And so began a relationship of ecstatic highs and agonizing lows. Paul Brown got the patent for re-inventing pro football but Blanton helped make it work. In the Browns' first 10 years from 1946-55 they won the league championship seven times and played in the championship game the other three years. Such domination was unprecedented.

Not only were they coaching colleagues, Paul Brown and Blanton Collier became close personal friends. Their families spent time together. Because the Colliers continued to live in Kentucky during the off-season, Paul and Katy Brown usually stayed with them for a few days while driving to Florida for their annual winter vacation. The families watched each other's children grow up. Stoic Paul Brown and Blanton's spirited daughter, Kay, played duets together on the piano. Laughter and music filled the air when the Brown and Collier families got together.

"Oh, we loved it when Paul and Katy came to visit," recalled Blanton's middle daughter, Kay Slone. "We couldn't wait."

Decades later, she wrote a book about her father, *Football's Gentle Giant—The Blanton Collier Story*. It included this ominous observation, "Paul Brown was my friend, my father's friend, my family's friend . . . I saw him as a kindly man, although I saw flashes of what was possible; what came later. The simple truth of the matter is this: We loved him, because Daddy loved him."

Over the years Collier received several job offers and almost automatically said no. He turned down the Baltimore Colts' head coaching job, which then went to Weeb Ewbank. Years later he turned down the Los Angeles Rams and Green Bay Packers.

But it was different when Collier got a call from the University of Kentucky. Blanton's undergraduate degree was from Georgetown, the tiny college near his Kentucky home, but he held a master's degree from the University of Kentucky and was well on his way to a doctorate there. Besides, the Kentucky campus in Lexington was a mere 19 miles from the Collier family's home in Paris. You can drive it in 15 minutes today.

Paul Brown, however, seemed unworried and readily granted permission for Blanton to talk to them.

"I'll simply make it so attractive for him financially that he'll have to stay," Brown confidently told the media. "I'd rather lose my right arm than lose Blanton Collier."

In retrospect, Collier's eight-year career at Kentucky was at least as intriguing as the decades he spent with the Browns.

It was hard to imagine Blanton Collier—ethical, moral and honest—coaching the University of Kentucky. In his tome, "Onward to Victory—the Crisis That Shaped College Sports," acclaimed college professor, researcher and author Murray Sperber portrayed the University of Kentucky in the early 1950s as one of the most corrupt college athletic programs in the country.

The Kentucky job opened because Paul (Bear) Bryant, who had

coached the Wildcats to their eight greatest football seasons ever, was on the run. He posted a 60-23-5 record from 1946 to 1953, but the NCAA was hot on his trail and he fled for Texas A&M.

Bryant was able to fly under the radar of the NCAA investigators until then because they were pre-occupied with Adolph Rupp's Kentucky basketball program. In the famous gambling scandal of 1951 in New York, five of Rupp's players were convicted of shaving points at the National Invitation Tournament (NIT) at Madison Square Garden. It was a far-reaching probe involving several college teams, but Kentucky was the headliner. After all, the Wildcats won three national championships in four years during that period.

Rupp's teams had quite a rap sheet. They were suspected of shaving points in 95 games over six years in the late 1940s and early 1950s, many of them at home, but no one outside of New York pursued the probe, certainly not in Lexington, the center of horse racing country, where gambling was a way of life. Professor Sperber pointed out that Rupp associated openly with Ed Curd, the most notorious gambler in Lexington, and even invited Curd along on trips with the team. The Wildcats were tainted and everybody in Kentucky knew it. Bookies in Lexington and Louisville refused to accept bets on college basketball in the 1949-50 season.

When the hammer came down, Rupp skated away clean but his players paid the price.

"The Chicago Black Sox threw ball games, but these kids only shaved points," Rupp said in their defense.

His arrogance only infuriated the NCAA, which gave Kentucky the "death penalty." Its entire basketball program was shut down for the 1952-53 season for various violations, including paying players. Kentucky played no varsity basketball games that season.

The NCAA then focused its attention on Bear Bryant's Kentucky football team. The Bear was not looking for that kind of exposure. He was guilty and he knew it. He resigned and took a job far away at Texas A&M. When the NCAA got interested in him there, he moved again to Alabama where he was elevated to sainthood.

In his memoirs, Walter Byers, executive director of the NCAA in the 1950s and 1960s, commented on Bear Bryant's recruiting methods. He would entice recruits with $20 bills—fifty at a time.

Obviously, Kentucky needed a savior. Adolph Rupp was entrenched as basketball coach. He wasn't going anywhere. They would continue to accommodate his methods because glory followed him. The new football coach, however, presented the opportunity to put at least one clean face on a high profile program. Blanton Collier was ideal. He was a local hero and he was pure as the driven snow.

Blanton wanted the job. His wife, Forman, wanted it even more. But Blanton needed the blessing of his mentor. He flew to Fort Myers, Florida, where Paul Brown was vacationing, and discussed the opportunity. Blanton had decided to take it. "Good luck," said Brown. Collier needed to hear that from his friend. Then he flew back to Cincinnati, drove the 60 miles south to Lexington, and on Feb. 11, 1954, he accepted the Kentucky job.

So, why did Blanton Collier even consider Kentucky?

"It was home," said his daughter, Kay Slone.

The Bluegrass State raised great racehorses but was not known for thoroughbred football players. In order to compete in the Southeastern Conference against such national powers as Tennessee, Alabama, Auburn, LSU and Georgia, Kentucky needed out-of-state players. It wasn't easy to get them because admission requirements for non-residents were strict and inflexible, even for blue chip football players. They had to rank in the upper half of their high school class. No exceptions. Blanton thought he had recruited Joe Namath and Dick Butkus, but the admissions office wouldn't accept them.

Blanton did not always agree but he abided by the policy. He went even further. He would not tolerate tutors writing papers for his players and he curtailed the practice of giving them sneak peeks at tests, which had caused such a contretemps at West Point a few years earlier. He patrolled attendance at mandatory study table for players whose academic work slipped below his standards. People said, "This is suicidal." Collier said, "No, this is education." Within a few years Bernie Moore, the commissioner of the Southeastern Conference, applauded Kentucky for leading the way in raising academic standards for athletes. The faculty grew to respect him and love him. He was quite unlike any other football coach they knew.

Kentucky became the classic example of a school trying to be Harvard on Monday through Friday and Oklahoma on Saturday. But on Saturdays the Wildcats still played like Kentucky. The administration felt the pressure from alumni, boosters and donors.

Collier lasted eight years and had an overall record of 41-36-3, not bad for a school playing a Southeastern Conference schedule.

Kentucky has had eight coaches since Collier and none left with a winning percentage. Shortly after the 1961 season, he wrote a letter to university president Dr. Frank Dickey advocating Kentucky's withdrawal from the Southeastern Conference because it never would compete. He suggested joining a conference with universities of similarly rigid academics. The unpleasant alternative, he said, was to lower its standards. Kentucky responded by lowering the boom. Collier was fired. For the first time in his life he was shown the door and the Collier family was bitter. But within a few days, their mood brightened.

While he was at Kentucky he had turned down head coaching offers from the Los Angeles Rams and the Green Bay Packers. Vince Lombardi wound up taking the Green Bay job. Blanton thought his home was in Kentucky, but it really was in Cleveland. Paul Brown called. It was time to come home. He rejoined the coaching staff of the Cleveland Browns. Coach Paul Brown had his right arm back.

In *The Plain Dealer*, Brown referred to Collier as "one of my closest friends."

Sadly, that would change a year later when Browns owner Art Modell fired Brown. Modell then turned to general manager Harold Sauerbrei and asked him who should succeed Brown.

"There's only one man," said Sauerbrei. "Blanton Collier."

Before accepting the job, Blanton once again asked for Brown's blessings. What could the fired coach say? "No, out of loyalty to me, refuse the job. You refused the Colts job. You refused the Rams job. You refused the Packers job. You owe it to me to refuse this one."

That's what Paul Brown felt. He had given Blanton his first opportunity in pro football in 1946 and he gave him his second chance just a year earlier. Brown was perceived as a cold, calculating man but waves of emotion were cascading over him at that moment. He was stunned. When Modell fired him, it came without warning. And then, to be replaced by his loyal assistant, that was humiliating.

But Paul Brown could say none of that. The rules of chivalry permitted him to say only one thing.

"Take the job. Good luck," he said to Blanton.

And that was the end. Paul Brown turned around, walked away and never looked back at his old friend.

The Browns won the NFL championship in 1964, Blanton's second year as head coach. It was the first Browns game I actually

8553

covered for *The Plain Dealer*. And I thought it would become an annual event, like the early fifties. Paul Brown's loyalists discredited Collier's achievement. "He won it with Paul Brown's players," they said. The record, however, showed that it had been nine years since Paul Brown won it with his players.

Blanton never won another NFL championship but he came close. In 1965 the Browns lost the championship to the Packers in Green Bay, 23-12. In 1968 and '69 they lost the NFL championship games, one game shy of the Super Bowl.

Those who played for him insisted that he knew more about coaching each position than the position coaches. He coached without anger, without ridicule and without raising his voice. His players revered and respected him. None of them ever poked fun at his hearing loss. Wide receiver Gary Collins came the closest.

"At the last team meeting before a trip to a playoff game, he reminded us about the dress code on the plane," Collins said. "I asked him about ties. Should we wear ties? 'No ties,' he said. 'Overtime.'"

Collier was so unlike those who coach today. He kept no secrets from the media. On the contrary, he wanted his reporters to understand the game and why things happened.

For example, in 1970 many things went wrong. There were injuries to key players. The Browns had trouble running the ball. One dark night in Pat Joyce's saloon, left tackle Dick Schafrath explained his theory about the demise of the running game. With Paul Warfield gone, he said, the running backs couldn't turn the corner on the famous Browns sweep. Warfield had the key block and he never missed it. Warfield had been traded to Miami the previous winter so the Browns could draft quarterback Mike Phipps from Purdue.

It sounded reasonable so I wrote a column on the subject. The next Sunday I was working the locker room, getting my post game quotes, talking to as many players as possible, when Blanton motioned me over to his tiny office, which was just off the main locker room in the old Stadium.

He liked my column, he said. He agreed with it, except for one minor point. I wrote that Warfield blocked the outside linebacker. No, said Blanton. Warfield blocked the cornerback. He then turned to a rollaway blackboard in his office and began drawing X's and O's. He added the squiggly lines showing who went where. He carefully diagrammed the play. I started to fidget. The players were getting dressed and leaving. Quotable nuggets were headed out into the dark Sunday night. But when the teacher is teaching, no one leaves the classroom. I felt honored. He gave me a private lesson.

Collier claimed he was the only one in the Browns' organization who stood up and opposed the trade of Warfield to Miami. Someone put the notion in Art Modell's head and there was no getting it out.

The Browns needed a quarterback. Bill Nelsen's knees were shot. He could barely walk. He strapped himself into heavy braces on each leg for practice and games. Even with these encumbrances, he was the best the Browns had and he wasn't bad. He took them to the NFL championship games in 1968 and '69, but his body was worn out.

The top two quarterbacks in the 1970 draft were Terry Bradshaw from Louisiana Tech and Phipps from Purdue, but the Browns didn't have a chance to get either one unless they traded up, way up. The Browns were drafting near the bottom of the first round.

Pittsburgh had the first pick in the draft and they were going to pick Bradshaw. Green Bay had the second pick and indicated they were not interested in Phipps. Miami had the third pick and they did not need a quarterback. The Dolphins were solid with Bob Griese and they were amenable to doing business with the Browns but Dolphins general manager Joe Thomas was a tough negotiator. The price for their third pick in the draft was Paul Warfield, the one player Collier did not want to trade. He then turned his attention to Phipps.

"I went down to Purdue and looked at films. I talked to their coaches. I talked to Phipps. When I left I didn't want to make the trade. There was something about him. Something was missing," Blanton told me later.

They sat down to make the final decision, Art and his front office sycophants in a room.

"I was the only one who voted against the trade," Blanton said.

It turned out to be a disastrous trade, maybe the worst in Browns history. The Browns gave up a Hall of Fame receiver, one of the best who ever played the game, for the rights to roll the dice and draft a quarterback who was not the answer.

With Warfield gone, Nelsen in leg irons and Hall of Fame running back Leroy Kelly afflicted with knee problems, the Browns struggled to a 7-7 record in 1970 and the beloved coach stepped down.

Blanton never surrendered hope of finding a cure for his deafness, which was labeled "inoperative nerve deafness." Sound got through, but it was scrambled, like pieces of a jigsaw puzzle rattling around in the box before you put it together.

By the late 1960s some medical advances had been made and Dr. Bill Lippy, an ear specialist in Warren, Ohio, was a leader in the field. Modell and Blanton made numerous visits to his office together. Modell often said that if a cure for deafness could be found, Collier would have been his coach for many more years.

Dr. Lippy did help. One day Blanton pulled into the garage of his home in the Cleveland suburb of Aurora with a new hearing device in his ear.

"I got out of the car and I heard a strange crackling sound," he recalled.

He went in the house and got his wife to come into the garage and identify the sound.

"That's the engine cooling off," she said. "All cars make that noise."

It was the first time Blanton ever heard it.

Dr. Lippy's hearing device was not a panacea, however. Collier knew he could no longer go on late in the first half of a Saturday afternoon game against the Dallas Cowboys on Dec. 12, 1970. The game was played in a steady downpour, which caused havoc with his hearing aids. The wires were drenched. He had no communication with his assistant coaches in the spotter's booth on the roof. His eyes in the sky were worthless.

"I took off the headset and turned the game over to Nick Skorich," he remembered.

He said he could only stand helplessly and watch Skorich make several tactical blunders as the Browns lost to the Cowboys, 6-2.

"I knew right then that Nick should not be a head coach," Blanton said. "Art gave him the job anyway when I retired."

Blanton died on March 22, 1983, of a nasty cancer that caused much suffering. The doctors and nurses did not understand his deafness. They could not communicate with him. They did not know how to ease his pain.

Meanwhile, his old friend, Paul Brown, remained distant.

After Blanton's death, his middle daughter, Kay Slone, resumed work on the book about her father that she had begun many years earlier. She set out to interview those who had relationships with him over the years. She interviewed 101 former players, students, coaches and friends.

Only one is missing.

She called the Cincinnati Bengals' office and asked for Paul Brown. In the book she detailed her efforts.

"I left my name and the subject of my book with the secretary. At her suggestion, I called the following week to check on an appointment. One call. Two calls. Three calls. The secretary was kind but embarrassed. Finally I wrote a letter. There was no response."

At last, she sent a long letter by registered mail, sweetly reminiscing about those happy hours they sat together on the piano bench in Paris, Kentucky.

He never acknowledged it.

The love was gone.

Doug Dieken:
"Holding, Number 73"

When he was a rookie with the Cleveland Browns in 1971, Doug Dieken didn't unpack his clothes during the first week of training camp. He kept his suitcase in his car and he kept his gas tank full, ready to go back home to Streator, Illinois, on a moment's notice.

"I didn't expect to make the team," he said. "In fact, I was cut in training camp. They put me on waivers, but they changed their mind before I could get out of town."

He never left. Dieken has now been with the team for 40 years, employed as an offensive left tackle from 1971 through 1984 and as the radio analyst since 1985. No one has been with the organization longer.

While organizing my newspaper files for this book, I discovered that I had written more articles and columns about the old left tackle than anybody I had ever covered. I counted at least 13, and some others probably got misplaced or got lost. I was astonished. I also did two radio commentaries about him and a television story on "PM Magazine." In the 1970s and '80s I turned Dieken into a beat because he was fun to write about. He had a quaint, self-deprecating sense of humor and he often found himself in wacky situations.

Younger Browns' fans know him only as the radio voice of the team, not realizing that he was the most colorful character in its history.

Consider, for example, his bizarre career at the University of Illinois.

"We were on probation my entire four-year career there because of an issue with a slush fund," he related when we got together to update his story.

"Yes, my career at Illinois was a beauty. My sophomore year we were 1-9. My junior year we were 0-10. As a senior we were 3-7. Add them up. I played in a total of four winning games."

That was bad but it could have been worse. Thankfully, Doug's freshman team played only two games.

"Back then freshmen were not eligible to play in varsity games. We were cannon fodder for the varsity in practice. But we actually scheduled two freshman games, one against the Purdue freshmen.

"We had a freshman punter on scholarship but he was hurt in a car wreck so I punted. I was very versatile.

"Our punt team never actually practiced. The coach said line up this way and block the man in front of you. Purdue lined up in the gaps, though, and we didn't have a plan for that. I had one punt blocked, another one tipped and they were penalized twice for roughing the kicker. Afterward the freshman coach said, 'That was the most courageous game by a punter I've ever seen.'"

That was typical of Doug. He always managed to get noticed. The pass-catching tight end was the team's most valuable player as a junior and senior and was considered one of the great receivers in the annals of Illinois football.

"I always considered that an indictment of our passing game," he said.

Some poor souls live a nine-to-five life. So does Doug. He goes 9 a.m. until 5 a.m. the next morning.

"After the football banquet my junior year we went to the bar where we usually drank and one of the townies sucker-punched the bartender who always gave us free beer. The brawl started inside the bar and spilled out on the sidewalk. I got hit in the head with a tire iron. The second time the police came, I had a towel around my neck to stop the bleeding. The police said, 'What happened to you?' I said, 'I picked a scab.'

"I spent the rest of the night in jail.

"The headline at the top of the page the next afternoon said, 'Dieken MVP.' A little lower another headline said, 'Dieken Arrested in Gang War.'"

His senior year was marked by a players' revolt, possibly the most effective rebellion in college football history, which Dieken orchestrated.

"I learned that they were going to fire our coach, Jim Valek, in the middle of the season, right after the Ohio State game," Dieken said. "I told the team. We lost to Ohio State and after the game we took a vote right there in the locker room. If he's not here Monday, we won't be here either. Everybody raised his hand. Valek was a good guy. We liked him. The administration backed off. They said they had misread the situation. The next game was Homecoming against Purdue. If they had fired him, there would have been no Homecoming Game because there would have been no team. Valek stayed. We played and we beat Purdue."

So this was the person I was dealing with, a mad man who would fall on a grenade for his coach and who would fight to the death in defense of the bartender who gave him free beer. Dieken wasn't just a character. He had character.

* * *

In a historical sense, Dieken was a big deal because he was only the fourth starting left tackle in Browns history. Jim Daniell was the first in the team's inaugural year of 1946. Coach Paul Brown fired him after one season when he got drunk and spent a night in jail the week before the league championship game. Tackle Lou Rymkus and wide receiver Mac Speedie were with Daniell and shared the cell with him, but Daniell was treated more harshly because he was the team captain.

The next year Chet Adams and Ernie Blandin alternated at the position but neither was considered the regular starter.

Hall of Famer Lou Groza was the second established starter. He held the position for 12 years (1948 to 1959) and returned for seven more years as the place kicker (1961 to 1967). Dick Schafrath was the third left tackle. He started for the next 12 years (1960-71).

The Browns certainly never expected that kind of longevity from Dieken when they picked him in the sixth round of the 1971 draft with the intention of converting him to left tackle. Dieken was a long shot. It was a hope, not necessarily an expectation that he could replace Schafrath, who was nearing the end of a brilliant career that saw him voted into the Pro Bowl six times.

"I'd played only a quarter of a game at tackle in my life before 1971," Dieken pointed out later. "That was in the Blue-Gray Game the previous winter."

Maybe that's what caught the eye of the Browns' scout. The coaches, however, failed to see the same potential on the practice field. Dieken was, after all, a lean, pass-catching tight end. He couldn't be expected to metamorphose into an offensive lineman overnight. When training camp ended in September, 1971, the Browns put Doug on waivers intending to hide him on the practice squad but the Miami Dolphins claimed him. Miami line coach Monte Clark had played right tackle for the Browns in the 1960s and he still had friends on the team. He called them for recommendations and they said, "Grab Dieken." The unheralded rookie was suddenly a hot commodity. The Browns withdrew his name from the waiver list and placed him on their active roster. He unpacked his suitcase and looked for an apartment.

In the seventh game of the '71 season, Bob McKay was hurt and Dieken started in his place at right tackle, a position Dieken had never played. His previous experience was at left tackle in parts of six quarters—two in pre-season games, three in the regular season and one in the Blue-Gray college all-star game. Surprisingly, he did well against Atlanta's all-pro defensive end Claude Humphrey and the coaching staff was pleased. Three weeks later he became the permanent starter at left tackle and the Browns won their last five games of the 1971 season and made the playoffs. He had big shoes to fill, replacing Schafrath. You don't merely win the left tackle job, you are anointed. Left tackle is the most important position on the offensive line because it protects the quarterback's blind side (since most quarterbacks are right handed). So here was Dieken, a wise-cracking rookie, not even a high draft choice, a lowly sixth-rounder, suddenly adorned in the garments of royalty. Who would guess that he would hold the job from Nov. 21, 1971, through the 1984 season, one of the longest tenures in pro football history?

*   *   *

One day I approached Doug in the locker room after practice and opened my notebook. "Tell me your life story," I said.

We didn't have much time, but what kind of a story could Doug have? His was a sterile existence. He was a young bachelor living in a one-bedroom apartment and he hadn't even voted in his first presidential election yet. I don't think he had a girlfriend, although it would not be prudent to make any assumptions along those lines, not even in retrospect.

He grew up on a farm in the middle of Illinois. He had two brothers, no sisters. His parents were comfortable, very comfortable. They were both college graduates, which was not typical in those days.

They owned grain silos and leased some of their land to tenant farmers. If their spread were any bigger, Edna Ferber would have written a book about them. It seemed that they owned half of central Illinois. People said their ZIP code was the biggest one in Illinois and it was all theirs. Privately, I wondered if he really needed this football job. Years later I realized that he did not. Doug did not get into all that. He said he was a farmer.

"My dad always said, 'Act like you make only half of what you make.' It's a good piece of advice," Doug said later.

He was not very interesting yet so I padded the story further down with some mundane information. Forgetting about his brothers, I inadvertently referred to him as an only child. Most people did not notice the disappearance of his two brothers in the space of a few paragraphs. They probably didn't even read that far. But Doug, unlike many linemen, could read and he confronted me the next time I was in the locker room.

"You killed my brothers," he said.

* * *

Doug quickly asserted himself, becoming the leader of the offensive line, which traveled in a pack on and off the field. Season after season, he never missed a game. Despite seven knee surgeries, he held Browns records for most consecutive starts and most consecutive games played when he retired.

"Why didn't you sit out a game now and then?" I asked him once.

"When you take the first day off, it's much easier to take the second day off," he said.

He was literally an iron man. While rushing out the door for a golf game, he noticed that he was wearing a wrinkled shirt. He didn't have time to change shirts, so he plugged in his iron and ironed it while he was wearing it. The imprint of the iron was visible on his chest for years.

"Don't ever try this at home," he cautioned. "In fact, don't try this anywhere. If your shirt is wrinkled, for God's sake, take it off."

He also "held" a dubious record. It was joked that his holding penalties if laid end to end would stretch for a mile. It was his trademark, but it was no joke. For much of his career, holding penalties were 15 yards and he averaged a dozen a year for 14 years. He stopped more Browns drives with his bare hands than opposing middle linebackers did. He had many multiple holding games. There were times he was the leading ground gainer for the other team. He hated anonymity and loved to hear his name announced over the PA system, "Holding, number 73, Doug Dieken." When he reached 1,760 yards the Bay Village service department painted a stripe a mile long on Lake Road that began in front of his house. He even had vanity license plates on his car that read, "ME HOLD." Grammar never was his strength. After he retired, he changed it to past tense, "ME HELD."

"Holding" may have been a punch line, but it also was an effective pass blocking technique and it saved the life of his quarterback many times. Doug described it as "absorbing" the onrushing defensive end in a bear hug and then backpedaling until they both tumbled to the ground. It was difficult to determine who was responsible: Did Doug pull or did the defensive man push? In either case, the defensive end was out of the play and the quarterback was out of danger. In the process, Doug's body took a terrible beating. He usually ended up on his back and on the bottom.

"I play football because it's the only thing I've ever done," he said once. "I'm just trying to earn my little way. When the day comes that I can't play, I don't know what I'll do. I'd hate to wake up on Monday morning and not be sore."

* * *

Along the way, Doug taught us many things. Foremost is, don't get into a practical joke contest with somebody who has unlimited time and unlimited money. I learned the hard way.

In the spring of 1980 Doug was the first person we knew who put humorous messages on a telephone answering machine. It was his off-season and he had nothing but time. I wrote about it, beginning with a poem:

> When the football season ends,
> Dieken says goodbye to friends.
> All day long he sits alone
> Playing with his Dictaphone.

He sits in his palatial home on the lake in Bay Village, surrounded by his memories and a few sticks of furniture. His only toy is his telephone answering system. Every morning he records a new message, recording it over and over until he gets it perfect. This takes him several hours.

One day he played a Johnny Cash album into the recorder, the one that begins, "Hi, this is Johnny Cash . . ." Dieken's voice then interrupted to say, "Hey, Johnny. Give me the phone."

Another day he was John Wayne. "Hello, pilgrim," he said in his best John Wayne impression. The background music was "God Bless America."

A few days ago, when he received his mail order ordination that made him a minister in a California church, he was the Reverend Doug Dieken. A rollicking gospel choir introduced his spiel. He is now licensed to perform functions of the clergy such as preaching, saving, counseling and marrying. If the Browns have a lousy season, he can preside at graveside services.

At the end of my column I suggested that everyone should call this lonely bachelor and leave a cheerful message. Conveniently, he was listed in the phone book. In the next four days, he got 600 calls, many from women who left their names and numbers and promised to make him happy. Any normal man would he grateful, but not Dieken. On the first day, Dieken's phone began ringing shortly after newspapers started landing on front porches. He called me.

"I got the first call at 6:30 this morning and my phone hasn't stopped ringing. Every time I get a call, you'll get one, too," he threatened.

He then recorded a message on his answering machine that said his number had been changed. The new number was mine.

Welcome to the game.

Not to be outwitted by an offensive lineman, I put my phone on call forwarding and bounced the calls back to Dieken. This became a vicious circle which must have been confusing, especially to women who wanted to show him a good time.

Subsequently, he recorded a new message inviting everyone to a party at my house, including directions. Radio station WMMS played the message on the air, guaranteeing a huge turnout. Each day Doug added a new twist and WMMS put it on the air. Bring spray paint for a graffiti contest. Bring shovels, there are a hundred silver dollars buried in the front lawn. If you know any Hell's Angels, bring them.

That Friday night I got home from work about nine o'clock. I walked in the front door and a hundred people were there and they had already broken the second floor toilet. Thankfully, they were smoking pot and drinking mostly whisky, not beer. The first guy I saw had a gun sticking out of the waistband of his pants. He turned out to be an off-duty cop.

For a while, everyone in town started going crazy. Alliances and truces were pledged and broken. When Maddy and I returned from our honeymoon, we discovered that Doug had paid a visit. He had glued mirrors on our bedroom ceiling and hidden bells between the mattress and the box springs. We sat down on the edge of the bed and it started ringing like the Good Humor Man's ice cream truck. Maddy said she wanted a Klondike Bar.

Dieken also put goldfish in every sink, toilet, bathtub and ice cube tray. Too bad for the fish, they did not survive.

When the Browns returned from a game against the Raiders in Oakland, Doug found that someone had left 12 chickens and a sack of feed in his garage all weekend with his new Mercedes-Benz sedan.

"The chickens were everywhere, especially all over my car," Dieken said through clenched teeth.

When Dieken was picked for the Pro Bowl in Honolulu he rendezvoused with ace homicide detective Dick Wilson who was on a temporary suspension from the Los Angeles Police Department for driving his motorcycle into the cocktail lounge of the Century Plaza Hotel at two o'clock in the morning.

Dieken arranged for Wilson to patrol the sidelines of the Pro Bowl with a photographer's pass.

"I had a Brownie, but he said it didn't look official enough so I had to borrow a professional Nikon," Wilson said. "He told me to get a picture of him every time he did something. The camera broke after only one picture. I was sorry about that. I could have gotten a lot of nice pictures of Brian Sipe and Dan Fouts running for their lives."

For Wilson, the rest of the week was a life-changing experience. Luckily for him, it lasted only one week.

"Trying to keep up with him for one more week would have killed me," Wilson said. "I have been involved in manhunts and stakeouts. I have chased the most perverse and degenerate members of society.

But let me tell you, a week with Dieken was a real education in depravity.

"He fixed me up with a different girl every night, one uglier than the next," said Wilson. "But at least they were prettier than the ones he went out with."

Who knew why Wilson would make such a statement? It was an outright canard. Dieken has never been seen in the company of a homely girl in his life. He was engaged to a knockout. He was married to a television beauty and they have two children, a daughter who is starting to resemble a Hollywood star and a son straight out of central casting.

*   *   *

Before signing off on old number 73, you should know that he is a multi-faceted diamond who has done far more good than evil. He works tirelessly for the Special Olympics and for foundations that cure diseases, especially those that affect children. He had a younger brother who was mentally challenged and suffered from epilepsy. When Doug was chairman of the Cleveland Epilepsy Foundation in 1981, he turned it into a full-time job.

"We have never had a chairman who worked as hard as Dieken," said Judy Lester, an administrator for the Epilepsy Foundation. "Nobody else in history was even close."

He once played Santa Claus at Parmadale, a home for emotionally troubled children.

"What do you want for Christmas?" he asked one teenager.

"Just give me my present so I can get the hell out of here," said the young boy.

Doug was immediately attracted to the kid.

After a rugged spring mini-camp during Forrest Gregg's coaching regime in the mid-1970s, Doug participated in a Ten-Mile Bike Hike for the Retarded in Akron.

"I was beat up and hung over," Doug recalled during our refresher interview earlier this year. "I was looking to slip out of the bike hike early until one of the ladies on the committee said, 'We have $400 bet that you'd finish 10 miles.' Oh, no. My heart sank. Then my luck changed. I got a tire stuck in railroad tracks. That should get me out of this, I thought. Suddenly a truck pulls up with another bike. I had to pedal all 10 miles."

Doug usually rounded up his teammates for many of these adventures, especially for the Special Olympics, Doug's most heart-felt commitment.

"After one of them, Robert Jackson, Tom DeLeone and Bill Cowher said, 'Tell me what time next year. We want to do it again.' That's the way it was with those guys," Dieken recalled.

Those were the Kardiac Kids, special players and a special era for the Browns. In 1983 Dieken was awarded the Whizzer White Award for community service, one of the most prestigious honors in the National Football League. Doug cherished the award even more than his Pro Bowl selection.

Art Modell: Debt Was Good

Everybody took Art Modell for granted and that was the problem. A couple of years before he moved the Browns to Baltimore, I asked him about his remaining years in the game. How many would there be? Did he envision himself getting out, leaning back and smelling the roses before he pushed up the daisies? Would he ever sell the team? We were only talking.

"This team is in no shape to be sold," he said.

For 30 years Art's references to his bankers became a running gag and nobody laughed louder than Art. He believed in debt. Buy now, pay later. Debt was good. In an era of perpetual inflation, his economics made sense. On more than one occasion, Modell had quipped that he gave coach Bill Belichick an unlimited budget "and he already exceeded it," but we didn't take him literally. Suddenly, however, I sensed that Art had serious financial problems. He didn't say that directly, but he hinted.

For the life of me, I didn't know why he would be in financial trouble. Years later I learned of his investments in movies, which is an easy way to lose millions. In 1965 during the filming of *The Fortune Cookie*, a movie based around the Browns that was shot in Cleveland, Art became friendly with director Billy Wilder and stars Walter Matthau and Jack Lemmon. Hollywood had a magnetic attraction to him. Unfortunately, Art did not have a piece of *The Fortune Cookie*, which was profitable. He invested in other movies that were not.

In 1970 he bought an amusement park in Gatlinburg, Tenn., about 30 miles south of Knoxville in the Smoky Mountains. He called it an amusement park but it had no rides. It was a collection of museum attractions—log cabins, saw mill, candle maker, general store, things like that. If you wanted a glimpse of Tennessee life 100 years ago, that was the place to go, if you could find it in the mountains. Years later Dolly Parton bought it and put in some roller coasters and it's now called Dollywood.

He also bought radio stations but made no money on them. In

retrospect we can now understand the stress he put on his check-book.

When he bought the Browns in 1961, he was 35 years old, brash and fearless. The price tag was $4 million at the time and they were worth $350 million when he moved them to Baltimore. Actually, he bought only 55 percent of the team and most of his initial invest-ment was borrowed but it seems impossible that his original loan wasn't paid off somewhere along the way. His share of the profits from the 1964 championship season alone should have been enough to pay off his debts. He never met a man he didn't buy a drink for, but even his bar bills were not insurmountable.

Oddly, Art's purchase of the Browns was an accident. Curly Mor-rison, a Browns' running back from the 1950s, claims responsibility. Curly became an ad salesman for CBS in New York and because of his Ohio connections he serviced the network's big advertisers in the Cleveland area, especially the tire companies in Akron. They were his most important accounts.

"Whenever I came to Akron, I always made a point to stop in the Theatrical Grille in Cleveland to find out what was happening. That's where the deal makers hung out. That's where I heard the Browns were for sale," said Morrison.

He learned that team president Dave Jones, who headed the group that bought the Browns from founder Mickey McBride in 1953, was the contact man. Jones was 74 years old. His three main partners in the ownership group, Ellis Ryan, Saul Silberman and Homer Marshman, were also up in years. They had been involved in Cleveland sports all their lives. Jones and Ryan had once been inves-tors in the Indians. Silberman and Marshman owned racetracks. At their age they decided to cash in their Browns holdings.

"We have a deal on the table already," Jones told Morrison.

"What's the price?" Morrison asked.

"Three million dollars," Jones said.

"I can get you $4 million," said Morrison.

"I can give you 30 days to bring your buyer to us," said Jones.

Morrison knew something the Browns' owners did not know. CBS had just agreed to a new television deal with NFL commis-sioner Bert Bell that would pay each of the 12 franchises an addi-tional $1 million per year. This dramatically inflated the value of the teams. None of the owners knew this yet.

The arrangement was that Morrison would get a 10 percent finder's fee if he delivered a new owner who would pay $4 million. Morrison flew back to New York to sell the Cleveland Browns. The clock was ticking and nothing was happening. Nobody seemed interested. Time was running out when Modell surfaced. He had been a degenerate pro football fan. His beloved Giants were not for sale but the Browns were the next best thing. He cobbled together his savings. He sold his little television production company. He borrowed. He brought in the Schaeffer Brewing Co. of Philadelphia as a silent partner. He still needed almost $2 million. In order to make the deal, Bob Gries, whose father was a minor shareholder in the Browns, agreed to sell his holdings and simultaneously buy back in at the new price. Gries wound up owning 42 percent of the Browns. Morrison walked off with $400,000. The sellers cleared $3.6 million. They had bought the team in 1953 from Mickey McBride for $600,000.

For Modell, this was an amazing piece of entrepreneurship. Starting from next to nothing, within 30 days Modell was the controlling partner in the Cleveland Browns.

In hindsight, it is apparent that the albatross around Art's neck was the Stadium and the deal he had signed with the City of Cleveland during Mayor Ralph Perk's administration in 1974 to take over the old gray lady.

It was said that Art's lease to manage the Stadium for 25 years was the most misunderstood contract in Cleveland history. Cleveland media muckraker Roldo Bartimole continually drove harpoons into Modell's hide in his monthly sheet, *Point of View*, claiming that Modell was fleecing the city. Roldo didn't make the accusation once and then move on. Oh, no. Roldo was chronic. He turned the Stadium into a campaign that ran for years. He did not have a wide readership, only a few thousand, but every CEO in town was on his subscription list. The names of several *Plain Dealer* editors also were on the list and they gave Roldo grudging respect. Over time this influenced *The Plain Dealer*, which began to question Art's "sweetheart" deal.

In 1977 first-term mayor Dennis Kucinich told properties director Pete Pucher to study the lease. Pucher went through the books, bills and receipts with Stadium controller Mike Poplar, who welcomed the audit. It took weeks. An independent auditor was brought in to corroborate Pucher's conclusions, which praised the deal as a bonanza for the city and vindicated Modell. It was so overwhelmingly favorable to the city that when the audit was over, Kucinich asked Modell to similarly manage the Cleveland Zoo and other city properties, such as the Public Hall. Modell declined, which was lucky for him. Taking over the Stadium was the dumbest thing he ever did, but he didn't know that yet.

Before Modell came riding to the rescue, the City of Cleveland was losing between $300,000 and $500,000 annually operating the Stadium, according to estimates at the time by Cleveland City Council. Opened in 1931, the Stadium was more than 40 years old and was a nightmare to maintain. Very little had been done over the previous four decades. Steel was rusting. The wooden roof was rotting. Mortar was crumbling. Every winter pipes froze and burst. Rats and mice gnawed through electrical wiring. Most of the urinals were original equipment and some of them actually flushed. Other than that, the Stadium was in move-in condition.

Essentially, Modell rented the Stadium from the city and subleased it to the Browns and the Indians. To do this he created a new company which he called the "Stadium Corporation." Art owned the Stadium Corporation almost entirely by himself. He owned only 55 percent of the Browns. Robert Gries owned about 45 percent. The teams paid rent to the Stadium Corporation, rent which was based on their attendance. When the Indians had lean years, and they mostly had lean years, Art had lean years. Nevertheless, he paid his obligations to the city. He paid rent to the city and, for the first time in years, it was able to make its bond payments on the Stadium. Furthermore, Modell committed to spending $10 million for improvements.

Desperate for tenants and events to keep the Stadium busy, Modell considered a professional soccer team.

The most consistent aspect to soccer in Cleveland is that nobody ever made money from it. Vernon Stouffer owned the Cleveland Stokers franchise in the United Soccer League in 1967 and lost $1 million. The team averaged fewer than 5,000 fans per game at the old Stadium.

The next year the Cleveland franchise was part of the merged North American Soccer League under owners Alva T. (Ted) Bonda and Howard Metzenbaum and they also lost $1 million, averaging

4,424 fans for 17 home games. That figure did not include a crowd of 16,205 for a July 10, 1968, exhibition match—they call them "friend-lies"—against Santos, the team from Brazil that featured the great Pelé. The Stokers won, 2-1, in a game that ended in chaos when Santos' apparent tying goal with 72 seconds left was disallowed for offsides. The TV replay indicated, however, that it was a legal goal.

Bonda and Metzenbaum cut their losses and folded the team after the 1968 season, as did half the league. What was left of the North American Soccer League plodded onward for many years with eight teams, including the New York Cosmos, who drew huge crowds at Giants Stadium.

In the 1970s, Modell considered giving soccer another chance. He thought about buying a franchise in the North American Soccer League. As a test case, he promoted a game between the Polish national team and the United States national team. He needed 25,000 fans to break even but drew only 17,000. During its time in Cleveland the Polish team was under constant armed guard—not to protect them, to prevent them from defecting. The Poles won easily, 3-1, over the U.S. Olympic team, proof that we were not yet ready for international competition, but that wasn't the point. The attendance was less than Modell hoped but it was enough to keep him interested.

Modell sought advice from Howard Collier, who was part owner of the Cleveland Cobras, a low-budget professional team that played at Finnie Stadium, Baldwin-Wallace College's football stadium in Berea. "We had two meetings," said Collier. "I said I don't think the league will make it. I said I wish I could give you another answer."

Modell appreciated Collier's candor. Collier was among six benev-olent investors who, for personal, family or friendship reasons, saved the Cobras and kept them afloat throughout the 1970s, knowing they would never make a dime. They wrote off losses every year. Collier always laughed that they should have had their heads examined. If Modell had re-introduced a major league team in this market, Collier and his partners would have been delighted. Modell prob-ably would have bought out their franchise as a gesture of good will and they could have saved themselves several more years of losses.

But Modell took Collier's advice and wisely steered clear of soccer.

To increase revenue, Modell installed 100 loges and to pay for them, he borrowed $5 million. It cost another $2 million to rewire and replumb the place. That's how it went. When there was a base-ball strike in 1981 and a football strike in 1982, revenue fell short and Art paid another visit to his friendly banker. To make ends meet, he tried rock concerts, tractor pulls, two Notre Dame-Navy football games and a high school football doubleheader. The Indians discov-ered that when they returned from long road trips, the Stadium field resembled the surface of the moon.

Gries questioned the accounting and sued Art, complaining that some Stadium Corporation expenses found their way onto the Browns' books, reducing the football team's profits. The Indians sued Art over similar issues. The legal dynamics were enervating and Modell suffered a serious heart attack. He had open-heart surgery and almost died.

By 1987 another new mayoral administration cast covetous eyes on the lakefront and stripped Modell of half of his parking lot on the east side of the Stadium to make room for the Inner Harbor, the Rock and Roll Hall of Fame and the Science Museum. The city was charging Modell rent for the parking lot and, good fellows that they were down at City Hall, they doubled his rent for half his space. Publicly, Modell said nothing. Privately, he was seething.

Poplar, the Stadium controller, appealed the tax hike to Bob Jacquay of the Cleveland law department.

"We're sorry," said Jacquay, "but the city has no money."

We didn't realize it then, but the Browns were as good as gone.

Meanwhile, the campaign to build a new ballpark for the Indians gained momentum. On the night that Hank Aaron broke Babe Ruth's all-time home run record in 1975, Baseball Commissioner Bowie Kuhn was at the Stadium Club in Cleveland speaking to the Indians' official booster organization, the Wahoo Club, stressing the importance of a new ballpark. Kuhn's successor as commissioner, Peter Ueberroth, brought the same message to the City Club in 1986. American League president Bobby Brown added to the cacophony when he came to Cleveland and said a small, cozy ballpark was pre-ferred for baseball.

"Cleveland will lose the Indians if they do not get a new ballpark," Brown said bluntly.

The issue wasn't how long Cleveland ownership could hold out on a shoestring. The issue was how much longer the other baseball owners would tolerate the situation. When teams came to Cleveland, their share of the gate receipts often did not even pay for their meals and hotel rooms.

Governor Richard Celeste talked about state funding for a new baseball park and other politicians nodded compliantly. Action was indiscernible but at least the Indians had many high-profile spokespersons. Modell had nobody speaking for him.

As early as 1984 political columnist Joe Rice wrote in the *The Plain Dealer*, "If Celeste produces a smaller stadium that lures away the Indians, Modell's prime tenant at Municipal Stadium, then Modell is left with two options: cancel his Stadium lease with the city or move the Cleveland Browns."

Hardly anyone took Rice seriously, which was a big mistake. Rice nailed it.

In 1985 a Domed Stadium Committee was formed and it seemed interested in architect Bob Corna's design of a six-sided dual-purpose stadium with a retractable roof which he called a Hexatron. Corna said the stadium, which would be shared by the Browns and Indians, could be built for $100 million.

"Mayor Voinovich liked the idea, but he was moving on. He was near the end as mayor and was running for governor," said restaurateur Mike Zappone, an important supporter of the plan. "Everything is timing. Politicians react to problems, they don't plan for the future. Especially in this town."

Zappone, who ran a thriving restaurant at West 117th Street and Lorain Avenue, was vice-president of the Cleveland Restaurant Association.

"It was now 1990. Mike White was the mayor and he was worried about the Convention Center," Zappone continued. "Well, the Hexatron would have solved all of their problems. It would be built north of the Mall above the Shoreway and above the railroad tracks. The old Stadium would be cleared for lakefront development. As Corna designed it, the Hexatron connected to the Convention Center and there were five hotels that connected to the entire complex."

There were other thought-provoking aspects to Corna's plan, such as extending the RTA Rapid Transit train to the IX Center in order to create a tangible link to downtown and running the tracks through the Hexatron and Cleveland State University. Corna's ideas seemed exotic at the time, but they were actually simple and practical.

"Because of the weather here, there is a limited time for tourism," Zappone continued. "With all of this connected by rail, you never had to go outside.

"Bob Corna had made a beautiful model of the entire layout. We tried to make an appointment to show the layout to Mayor White but to get to White we had to go through Nate Gray and Ricardo Teamor. We go in. They looked at me like I was from the moon. They let us talk for five minutes. That was it. They never let us in to see Mike White. If you weren't a big player like Dick Jacobs, Bart Wolstein or Sam Miller, you didn't get an audience. In company like this, not even Modell was a big player. The Hexatron went away. It disappeared."

So did Mike White, Nate Gray and Ricardo Teamor. They all went away. White was exiled to an alpaca farm in Tuscarawas County. Gray and Teamor, White's bagmen and longtime personal friends, went to prison for bribery and extortion. They were City Hall's version of the triple crown.

The Indians finally got Jacobs Field, their cozy baseball park, in 1994 and their future was secured. The entire American League rejoiced. That same year Gordon Gund got his downtown arena in order to move the Cavaliers from Richfield in Summit County. Wasn't it hypocritical to raise so much hell about Baltimore stealing the Browns from Cleveland when Cleveland stole the Cavs from Summit County?

In 1994 Modell was left with the 64-year-old Stadium on the lakefront, where the winter winds blew off a different part of the roof every year, and it was all his for 10 football games per year. With the baseball team and its 81 dates gone, it was impossible to maintain the Stadium. Mayor Mike White and other city officials were silent. They had taken care of the Indians and the Cavs. They took the bows and accepted the praise. There was nothing left for Modell. The old Stadium was good enough for him and his customers. He was expected to pay his rent and pay the cost of maintaining it. He said nothing.

Actually, Modell had addressed all of this hypothetically in 1988.

"If the Indians go ahead with a Stadium of their own, I would be perfectly happy staying where I'm at," he said. "But I'd want some economic relief for the improvements I've made in the Stadium and the loss of my principal tenant. At this time, I wouldn't take the Indians or anybody for granted, and that includes the Browns."

That was more than a hint. It was a warning. What the city did to Modell was outrageous, unethical and immoral. The city stole Modell's prime tenant from him and gave him no compensation. It was pure theft.

The Indians were the team that wasn't in pennant contention for over 30 years. Worse, they didn't try for 30 years. Ownership never had the financial weapons to compete in the Big Leagues and such ineptitude was rewarded with a brand new ballpark, one of the finest ones in all of baseball.

On the other hand, the Browns under Modell had won one championship and were one victory away from the Super Bowl five times. Modell tried. His reward was the back of the hand across his face. The costs of maintaining the Stadium from the revenue of a dozen football games a year were insurmountable.

I asked Modell once if he thought the city would ever give him a new stadium now that the Indians had been accommodated.

"They have no money," Modell said tersely, quoting Mr. Jacquay in the Law Department.

Modell also had no money. Coach Bill Belichick was spending like a drunken sailor on a three-day pass. For example, he tore up the practice field less than a year after it had been re-sodded. In 1994 he signed free agent players to more than $20 million in signing bonuses. Modell went to his usual banks but this time they were cautious. He had gone far beyond his previous debt limits. They were afraid of him defaulting.

"Why don't you go public and reveal your predicament?" I said.

"Nobody will believe me," he said.

"That's not entirely true. Business people would believe him," said Zappone. "They would have rallied around him."

But Modell was partially right. He had lost the fans. Over a period of many years the fans spread the myth that Modell was cheap and the label stuck. I don't know how that ever got started because he was one of the most charitable people in Cleveland. He was a sucker for a sob story.

Modell had a bigger problem. His coach Bill Belichick turned the fans against him and his team by clumsily firing quarterback Bernie Kosar in the middle of the 1993 season. The reaction was unprecedented. The word "nuclear" comes to mind. Kosar was one of the most popular players in team history. He led the Browns to the AFC Championship Game three times. Injuries had taken their toll and he was not playing well, but it was no time to make a change at quarterback. The Browns did not have a competent replacement. The backup, Vinny Testaverde, was hurt and the third-stringer, Todd Philcox, lacked experience. Releasing Kosar at that time appeared impulsive, vengeful and disrespectful. The Browns had a 5-3 record when Kosar was released. They had a 2-6 record afterward.

Kosar was picked up by the Dallas Cowboys as an emergency quarterback for the rest of the 1993 season, but he hardly ever played. It was the same story the following year with the Miami Dolphins. And then Bernie was done.

Only the move of the Browns two years later ignited a bigger explosion. The day after Kosar was released three ladies from the Akron area set up a picket station on the sidewalk in front of the Browns' complex in Berea with signs denouncing Belichick. They were there the rest of the week.

The Browns' next home game was Nov. 21, 1993, and 71,668 almost booed Belichick off the field. The coach's relationship with the city was established.

After games many fans refused to leave. At least a thousand of them crammed shoulder to shoulder in the lower concourse outside the Browns locker room chanting, "Bill Must Go." During his painful post-game press conferences the angry mob almost drowned out the coach. The elephant was standing in the middle of the room. This was the atmosphere after every home game the rest of the 1993 season.

There were serious concerns for Belichick's safety. The coach and his wife were booed out of a restaurant in Brecksville, unable to eat their dinner. Brecksville police set up a command post in their driveway and provided round-the-clock protection for several months.

The following year was a fluke. Testaverde and Mark Rypien got the Browns into the playoffs, but it was a joyless accomplishment because the coach was sullen and unhappy. The entire franchise was gloomy. Even Art was glum.

I was still in denial early in the 1995 season when rumors out of Baltimore claimed the Browns were moving there. Frankly, I thought that before something like that actually happened Modell would issue an ultimatum to the city and catastrophe somehow would be averted. There is a process. Things such as this require a period of panic, suffering, agony, negotiation and resolution.

In September I ran into Dave Hopcraft in the Stadium Club. He was the former *Plain Dealer* editor who was working for Modell as a public relations man.

"He's moving to Baltimore," Hopcraft said.

I found that hard to believe. In the first place, why would Hopcraft divulge such devastating information that his boss clearly was not prepared to announce? It was such an incredible leak that I couldn't take it seriously.

By November rumors of the move were like a tsunami, building strength and speed. On Thursday, Nov. 2, 1995, a Washington television station interviewed me live on the air via satellite from the Browns' practice field in Berea.

"I can't believe the rumors are true," I said. "It's inconceivable that the Browns are moving to Baltimore."

The next Monday, Art Modell stood on a wooden podium constructed in a Baltimore parking lot and confirmed the inconceivable. When he finished thanking the mayor of Baltimore, the governor of Maryland and his new bankers, he sat down next to his old friend Al Lerner.

A few days later John Steadman, 67, the revered sports columnist in Baltimore who had scoffed at the rumor until the carpenters started building the podium, wrote the words those of us in this business should never forget. "Never discredit another man's story. He might be right," Steadman wrote.

Three years later Mike Trivisonno predicted on his WTAM radio show that Al Lerner would be the owner of the Cleveland Browns expansion team.

"Unlikely," I said. "Lerner isn't even a candidate."

When the NFL announced that it would auction off the new Cleveland franchise, several investors stood up and identified themselves. Among them were:

- Brothers Charles and Larry Dolan, native Clevelanders. They were the first ones to identify themselves and tell their stories. They looked like the favorites. Larry headed a law firm in Geauga County. Charles lived in New York and owned the New York Knicks, New York Rangers, Madison Square Garden, Radio City Music Hall and other high profile properties in New York.

- Cleveland real estate and construction mogul Bart Wolstein, who once owned the Cleveland Force, a major league indoor soccer team.
- Tom Murdough, the toy manufacturer in Streetsboro, Ohio.
- Howard Milstein, a wealthy New Yorker with no previous ties to Cleveland. He was obsessed with owning a pro football team, but other NFL owners were skeptical about him because legal squabbling over the family's $5 billion fortune looked like a tag team match. Two years later the league owners asked him to withdraw his $803 million bid for the Washington Redskins because they were not comfortable with his financing and they didn't like his style.
- Indians' owner Dick Jacobs who had already decided to sell his baseball team but hadn't told anybody yet.
- Al Lerner, who announced his candidacy at a press conference at the Wyndham Hotel in downtown Cleveland in August, 1998, two months before the NFL owners held their auction. He sat at a raised dais alongside Cleveland Mayor Mike White, Edward DeBartolo family lawyer Carmen Policy and Bernie Kosar. This was the first time the mayor had endorsed a candidate.

"Six months after the Browns left, Al and I began back channel discussions," White said.

I almost fell off my chair. Mike White came right out and said it. He used the words "back channel discussions." It was a typical Cleveland backroom deal. White and Lerner had made a secret pact. The auction was a farce. White could name his owner and the NFL would accept it because Cleveland had already begun construction on a stadium which would be the city's gift to the NFL. White had sold his soul to Lerner, Cleveland sold its soul to the NFL. I felt dirty being in the same room with these guys.

Kosar had been brought aboard only to sanitize Lerner, whose tainted image needed a complete makeover because of his role in Modell's move to Baltimore. Lerner helped set it up and flew his good friend to Baltimore for the announcement. Before Lerner could be taken seriously, it was necessary to distance himself from Modell. That marked the end of their friendship. Modell endorsed the Dolans' candidacy.

Carmen Policy, a lawyer from Youngstown who once represented Mafia criminals, was Lerner's football expert because he worked for the DeBartolo family as an attorney for the San Francisco 49ers. He was an odd choice to set up a football operation but he set up a slick deal for himself. He was given a $50 million stake in the expansion team.

The other groups were more logical. The Dolan brothers brought in Don Shula, the former coach and general manager of the Miami Dolphins, to set up their football organization. In Miami his Dolphins played in four Super Bowls, winning two of them back to back. Earlier in his career he also coached the Baltimore Colts to the Super Bowl, which they lost to Joe Namath's New York Jets.

Bart Wolstein's football expert was Hall of Famer Jim Brown, the greatest running back of all time.

Milstein brought with him former Browns players Paul Warfield and Calvin Hill. Warfield, another Hall of Famer, actually had front office experience with the Browns in the 1980s.

The bidding came down to Lerner and the Dolan brothers. When the price exceeded $500 million, the Dolans dropped out. Lerner, whose bottomless vault was lined with the tears and misery of MBNA credit card holders who had been sucked dry by usurious fees, won the franchise for $535 million.

Shamefully, after a three-year interval, the new team adopted the Browns' name and colors, as though nothing had happened, soiling the glorious 50-year tradition of the original Browns. It was my preference to retire the name and revere its memory. What masqueraded as a pro football team in Cleveland was a new franchise with no connection to the original.

The Lerner operation, clueless about running a pro football team, set back the expansion franchise at least 11 years. When Mike Holmgren was hired as president in January 2010, the organization was starting over for the fourth time. Had the Dolan brothers owned the team, Shula probably would have had the Browns in the Super Bowl within 10 years.

The expansion Browns were a fiasco in every aspect. The Cleveland fans, desperate for a new team, genuflected in slavish supplication to the NFL and they got what they deserved. The NFL kicked them in the teeth.

The Cleveland taxpayers rushed to completion a stadium that can be used only 10 times a year for pro football and perhaps for an occasional international soccer game and the odd college game. Nearby cities such as Detroit and Indianapolis have domed stadiums, but not Cleveland. Because of that, Cleveland is not qualified to bid for the state high school football playoffs much less a Super Bowl or any future Big Ten championship game.

Sadly, misfortune befell three of the four persons who sat on that dais in the Wyndham Hotel in August 1998.

Al Lerner developed a brain tumor and died in 2002 at the age of 69.

Mayor White did not run for re-election in 2002 and, at the age of 51, mysteriously left politics. He moved to Newcomerstown in Tuscarawas County, 85 miles south of Cleveland, and bought an alpaca ranch with his political campaign funds.

By age 46 Bernie Kosar filed for bankruptcy, his wife divorced him and he struggled with the effects of several concussions he incurred while playing football for the Browns.

Carmen Policy was 62 when he cashed in his $50 million equity in the Browns and trotted off to California wine country to grow grapes. He risks death or injury from earthquakes.

Art Modell was 75 when his Baltimore Ravens won the 2001 Super Bowl. Three years later he sold his interest in the team and retired to Palm Beach, Florida. His final ambition was induction into the Pro Football Hall of Fame, which never will happen. Browns fans will never permit such a ceremony to take place in nearby Canton.

Woody Hayes: Warrior Without a War

Ohio State football coach Woody Hayes was asked once, "Is winning the most important thing?"

"No," he said. "The greatest thing in life is hope."

He thought a great deal about hope. It's even engraved on his tombstone.

"In the night of death, hope sees a star. And listening, love hears the rustle of a wing," it says.

According to the old coach's interpretation, the star is the hereafter; the wing will take you there. Woody's up there somewhere. He was too good a man to be anywhere else.

Woody Hayes was more than a football coach. He was a tenured professor and he was paid like one. When college football coaches were starting to make hundreds of thousands of dollars a year, Woody turned down raises and was content with 40 grand. He was a football coach on Saturdays. He was a teacher every day.

Every Sunday afternoon, for example, Woody conducted class with all freshman football players which he called "Word Power." It was vocabulary class. He did not want his players to embarrass themselves, their school or their coach by talking like morons.

Cleveland lawyer Jim Conroy, a center on Woody's 1968, '69 and '70 teams, recalls one of the great coach's finest hours and saddest days.

"It was the last week in April, 1970," said Conroy. "Spring practice was over. We had just played the spring game. I got a message at my fraternity from Woody's secretary, Carol Sweda. The coach wants to see you. Whoever took the call put the note on the bulletin board. My heart dropped. What did I do wrong? There was a big party after the spring game. I didn't do anything wrong, but what did he *think* I did?"

Conroy had never been in Coach Hayes' office because he was never recruited. He was a walk-on. He had a morning class at nine

o'clock and was in Coach Hayes' office on the third floor of St. John
Arena by 10:30. What struck him was the simplicity of the office. It
was utilitarian—linoleum floor, metal desk, chair, movie projector
and a couch, the type that made him think of a psychiatrist's office.
Woody sometimes slept in his office. Carol ushered Conroy directly
into the coach's office.

"Jim," he said, "you're one of our better students."

Actually, Conroy led the team with a 3.75 GPA. How many major
college football coaches know the grade point averages of junior
walk-ons? Woody Hayes probably was the only one. But Woody did
not summon him to talk about his grades.

"I'm very concerned about campus protests, that they might shut
down the university," Hayes said. "These are violent times."

College campuses from coast to coast were throbbing with
turmoil over the Viet Nam War. Student demonstrations already
had forced the closing of some schools. College presidents had been
held hostage in their offices. The SDS—Students for a Democratic
Society—was the most radical of the protest groups and it had a
foothold at Ohio State. Outside agitators and organizers had come
in. The SDS was against the war, against the president, against Dow
Chemical, against the status quo in America and against soap and
water. They were scary.

Football coaches were the last people on earth to understand the
differences between long-haired hippies, antiwar protesters, Com-
munists, druggies, traitors and other antisocial types. In October of
1969 Ohio State assistant coach Earle Bruce flicked off the lights and
turned on the projector for the team's traditional Friday night movie.
That was one of Bruce's jobs. He picked the movie. The movie he
picked was *Easy Rider*, which lionized long-haired, leather-jacketed
hippies meandering mindlessly on their motorcycles. Woody almost
had a heart attack.

"Woody fired Earle from the job of picking the movies," recalled
Conroy. "That was just one of the times he fired him."

The Buckeyes, however, were not adversely affected. The next day
Ohio State easily rolled over Minnesota, 34-7.

In the spring of 1970, however, Students for a Democratic Society
were not a movie. They were real. Conroy says Woody wanted to
know more about them. He wanted a scouting report on the SDS.

"Woody asked me, 'What are their beliefs and philosophy?' I said

I didn't know. Then he said, 'That's the reason I brought you over. I want you to infiltrate their ranks.' He wanted me to find out what books they read and who influenced them. He wanted me to go to the bookstore and get those books for him."

Conroy was dumbfounded. He was in advanced Army ROTC. He actually wore his army uniform to classes and for marching drills. He had already taken his oath, which was the commitment cadets made when they entered their third year of officer candidate school. He was not the most likely person to infiltrate the SDS. But duty called. He hung up his ROTC uniform in his closet and went underground.

"I'd go up to a group of them and ask how I could understand all this. They gave me a list of well-known books by Eldridge Cleaver, H. Rap Brown and Jerry Rubin. I went to the bookstore and checked them out. I felt really embarrassed in the cashier's line. I was afraid somebody would recognize me and see the books I was buying. How could I have explained that? I kept them in the bag they came in and took them to Woody's office. Mission accomplished," said Conroy.

Hayes voraciously read the books and digested the information. Then he went out to confront the enemy on the Oval, a grassy area about 300 yards in diameter in front of the administration building. The radicals, as many as 2,000 at a time, held rallies there. They even set up a microphone and loud speakers. Woody said he intended to use their own equipment to talk some sense into them.

Tensions had reached explosive levels. Bob Trapuzzano, a defensive back from western Pennsylvania, sat at the base of the flag pole in front of the administration building with his German shepherd on a leash, guarding the American flag.

"I'll be damned if they're going to take this flag down," he declared.

Woody's players begged him to stay away from the Oval and avoid a confrontation.

"It was at night. It was dark. It was dangerous. He could have been roughed up," Conroy said. "But he was determined. So several of us from the team mingled in the crowd to make sure nothing happened to him.

"He pleaded with them not to shut down the university, that it was contrary to all principles. He was impassioned. He used football analogies. They thought, 'What is he talking about?' Coach Hayes and an English professor—who was from England—were the only professors I know who went out to the Oval and spoke to them."

Woody was a great orator, but this was one audience he could not reach. A conservative, a Republican, a Nixon supporter—Hayes had three strikes on him when he stepped to the microphone. They ignored him, which was fortunate considering the alternatives.

The following Monday, May 4, the Ohio National Guard opened fire on students at Kent State University, killing four and wounding nine, and every public college in Ohio was closed, including Ohio State, as well as many others across the country. The war between the establishment and the radicals suddenly had a body count.

"A week later Ohio State reopened with the National Guard surrounding the Oval with loaded rifles," said Conroy.

Woody's heart was broken.

Several years later he was asked to deliver the commencement address at Ohio State's spring graduation. He began by saying, "This is the greatest day of my life." And then he began crying tears of joy.

He ended his speech with the Greek expression, "Demos kratia—people rule. You have the ability to make it a better place."

He finally came out of the closet. He was a Democrat.

* * *

Eleven years later, in October 1981, Woody consented to an interview. It was a quieter time in his life. I met him in his office on the second floor of the ROTC Building and we spent much of the day together. He was thin and sick. He had undergone a tough gall bladder operation and there were complications. But he was no less dynamic. I drove back that night to *The Plain Dealer*, sat down at my typewriter and didn't leave until I had finished this story, which took first place in the annual Associated Press state sports writing competition:

The Plain Dealer
Monday, Nov. 2, 1981

Columbus—The four-wheel drive van, custom-painted in scarlet and gray, surged through freeway traffic in Columbus with Woody Hayes behind the wheel.

As two lanes merged into one, the scarlet and gray van asserted itself and a sedan was forced to give ground. It better give ground. Woody Hayes drives as he coached—straight ahead and others get the hell out of the way.

The passenger looked at the coach, now gaunt and gray, the result of his recent infirmities, looking all of his 68 years, and was moved to remark about Hayes' place in history.

"Ohio has produced seven presidents of the United States . . ."

"Eight presidents!" Hayes interrupted.

All right. All right. Eight presidents. You don't argue with Woody Hayes about history.

"Eight presidents," the man continued, "and here in Ohio, you will be remembered as a greater hero and with more affection than any of the eight."

"That's a lot of bull," said Ohio's greatest hero.

Somebody changed the subject and a hatchback barely got the hell out of the way.

* * *

In many ways, Woody Hayes is a beautiful person. First, his impulsive honesty is unassailable. It also is what made him the most controversial football coach who stalked the sidelines. What he said and what he did sometimes made even his dearest friends and most loyal supporters cringe. But if ever a man was genuinely honest, that man is Woody Hayes. He stands alone, a block of granite in a plastic world.

But he did tell a little white lie.

It was suggested Hayes misses coaching. In one sense, it is a moot point because his health probably would not permit him to coach this year. He underwent gall bladder surgery last spring and, a short while later, had to go back under the knife to retrieve a sponge that had been left in him.

They went back through the original scar and that's what took the starch out of him. He is some 60 pounds under his coaching weight. He is regaining his strength slowly, like an 80-yard drive in 25 plays. He fatigues easily and still hasn't regained his robust complexion. But he is recovering.

"No," he argues. He emphatically does not miss coaching. "I coached long enough," he says. "How many have lasted 45 years?"

He was not convincing. One can only suspect that he has gone through hell since he was summarily fired after hitting Clemson's Charlie Bauman in the Gator Bowl in December 1978. Only this year has he begun attending Ohio State games as a spectator, this noble spirit relegated to the press box, where he sits amongst many of his antagonists.

Hayes never had a great regard for sportswriters, who annoyed him by persistently trying to pry into areas he believed were none of their business. In his mind he carefully measured the public's right to know against his football team's right to privacy and found he had a clear conscience when he locked the gates of his practice field and the doors of his locker room.

"The reason I never wanted my players quoted in the papers," he explained, "is that it makes them soft. When you see a player talking his head off in the papers, you see a player getting soft."

You rarely saw Ohio State football players go soft.

* * *

Hayes is not going soft, either. For a man whose gait is slowed almost to stop-action and who negotiates stairs with painful precision, he maintains a mercurial schedule.

For example, on June 13, two days after being released from the hospital following his second operation, he flew via helicopter to Oxford for a reunion of the 1950 Miami University football team which he had coached.

"That's the team that got me my job here at Ohio State," he recalls. "We beat Sid Gillman's University of Cincinnati team. It was between Gillman and me for the Ohio State job. When we beat Cincinnati, I got the job."

Hayes is unrelentingly loyal to his former players. His doctors advised against the trip to Oxford. One of them even accompanied him on the helicopter flight. But if the trip darn near killed him, he never let it show.

His date book is loaded with so many speaking engagements, one would think he is running for office. Within one week last month he gave speeches at the Ashland College homecoming, to a group in Chicago and to another group in St. Louis. He fights off boredom by keeping busy. He'll stay busy if it kills him.

Ohio State gave him an office in, appropriately, the ROTC building, just to the north of his beloved football stadium. He can see the stadium from his office window. He is surrounded by bookcases, gorged with volumes on football, history and specifically military history.

A typical moment. A familiar face peers through the door. Wick Murray, doctor of history, military enthusiast, invites Hayes to attend his upcoming lecture on the German Luftwaffe in World War II. They briefly discuss the Luftwaffe's survival rate on the Russian front compared to the western front. Hayes, however, has a conflict. He is giving a lecture the same afternoon. Dr. Murray will send his syllabus for the course to Hayes instead.

At the moment, Hayes is researching another critical phase of World War II, the decision which, he claims, changed forever the course of the war. He explains that in May 1940, the Nazis had the French and English troops on the run, but Hitler ordered the advance through France halted short of the end zone, allowing 750,000 English and French troops to escape at Dunkirk—troops who returned to fight again.

Was this Hitler's decision solely, or did the generals agree? Hayes interviewed Field Marshal Erwin Rommel's son, who is now the mayor of Stuttgart, West Germany. From Rommel's son, Hayes learned Rommel agreed because the sprint through France had outrun the strike force's support units. The advancing troops were low on fuel and rations.

* * *

Hayes also is working on his next book, titled, *Football, History and Woody Hayes*. On a blackboard that consumes half of one wall in his office, is the outline for the book. Four chapters remain to be written, to be finished when his energy returns.

"The writing has to be just right," Hayes says. "It has to flow."

Later, sitting in his van, he reads passages from two completed chapters. They flow. Yes, they do, in a distinctive literary narrative. Within single chapters, they traverse both geography and time with dexterity. The flow at times is gentle, revealing a facet to his personality he has tried to hide. Here is a man of many skills.

For example, one chapter begins on a Saturday afternoon in New Philadelphia not long ago with Hayes and his wife, Anne, shopping for furniture for his cabin.

Suddenly, the narrative segues to Saturday night in New Philadelphia, but the year is 1941 and Jimmy Haverfield is walking along the main street, wearing his navy uniform. In a few weeks he reports to his assignment on the battleship U.S.S. Arizona moored at Pearl Harbor, where he becomes the first former Ohio State football player to die in World War II.

The author's range is breathtaking.

Another chapter:

Woody and Anne are vacationing in Montreal in the summer of 1954. His quarterback, John Borton, is on a navy cruise and due to put in at Montreal. It is now 1759 and British general James Wolf is victorious in the Battle of Quebec on the Plains of Abraham, stunting the French influence in North America and establishing English dominance on the continent. There are complaints that Wolf is a madman at worst, an eccentric at best, and the King of England muses that perhaps Wolf should bite the other generals and infect them with the same madness.

That is Woody Hayes' type of general. It is recalled that similar criticisms were directed at Hayes.

* * *

Hayes coached football like generals fought battles. Loose lips sink ships. Hammer at attack points on the line of scrimmage. Strength against strength. Trench warfare. Hand-to-hand combat.

He lived for the conflict. Indeed, he loved his adversaries because without adversaries there would be no conflict.

Above all, perhaps, he loved Bo Schembechler because Schembechler, the University of Michigan football coach, was his most revered adversary.

Woody recalls waking up in his hospital room after his second recent surgery and seeing a beautiful woman sitting at the foot of his bed.

"I wondered where I was," he said, allowing for the possibility he had died and woke up in heaven. "It was Millie and Bo Schembechler."

* * *

He developed a love-hate relationship with his Rose Bowl coaching rivals in the Pacific Eight, later the Pac-10. He recalled the furor he provoked on his first visit to Pasadena when he beat Southern California, 20-7, in the Rose Bowl on Jan. 1, 1955.

"You know," he said, "you sportswriters put a person in the position where they have to lie. Well, I could have lied, but I told the truth. I said there were four or five teams in the Big Ten that could have beaten Southern California."

It took a few years for that one to die down and by the time Hayes got out of coaching, there wasn't one team from the Big Ten, much less four or five, that could beat Southern California or any other team in the Rose Bowl. Hayes' rivals from the west coast rose up and beat him regularly and he loved them for it.

"There are three reasons for the emergence of the Pacific Coast Conference," he contends. "The first is the junior college system in California. That's where the great black players, who don't have the grades to get into a four-year college, go to get their grades up.

"Tom Hamilton, who happens to be a Columbus native and who played fullback at Navy in 1926, strengthened the entire league when he was the commissioner of the conference.

"And then there were the coaches—John McKay, Red Sanders and Len Casanova. They raised the quality of football so much."

* * *

Hayes loved a battle. In 1961 he took on the head of the Ohio State alumni association and beat him. Hayes contends the alumni director, now deceased, orchestrated the faculty committee that voted against sending the Buckeyes to the Rose Bowl following Ohio State's unbeaten 1961 campaign. It was a vendetta, Hayes maintains, to force him out. Woody's antagonist was formidable. The alumni director controlled alumni funds and decided where they would be spent.

Not only did Hayes win the power struggle, he was instrumental in creating the President's Club, which has raised $107 million over the last 20 years.

Now Hayes thinks of other adversaries. He speaks of Abraham Lincoln and Lincoln's rival for the 1860 presidential nomination, Stephen A. Douglas.

When it was apparent that Douglas, a Democrat, would not defeat the Republican Lincoln, Douglas traveled through the South speaking against abolition, attempting vainly to hold the country together. At Lincoln's inauguration, Douglas sat next to him, holding the President's stovepipe hat.

"And then," Hayes said, his voice cracking with emotion and fighting back tears, "Douglas went back to Illinois and died the following year from the cancer he had been suffering from."

Lincoln and Douglas, Woody and Bo. Woody and McKay. Woody and any of his adversaries.

"I played at Champaign 14 times," Hayes said, recalling those visits to the University of Illinois. "Now, as Dizzy Dean said, 'It ain't bragging if you done it.' We beat them 14 times because the week before each game we lived Abraham Lincoln. We used him as a symbol. We personalized him. We'd talk about him from the standpoint of his personal hardships, his loneliness. Kids today think they're lonely. Lincoln was a melancholy man. He could sense the loneliness of another man."

Hayes voice cracked again and he fought back tears. He is one of the most emotional, nostalgic men who ever lived and now his visitor sensed that, like Lincoln, he is lonely. He has no assistant coaches to admonish, no miscreant players to correct, no sportswriters to intimidate. He has no adversaries. He is a soldier without a battle. He is a general without an army. What could be lonelier than a warrior without a war?

For 28 years Woody Hayes was a tough man to live with because he demanded perfection.

"I believe in the great things in people," he said. "I believe in the great strength that is in people. It has to be tapped."

It may have been tough to live with him, but it is tougher to live without him.

"One thing you were not," his visitor said, "you were never dull."

His eyes twinkled. Damn right, he seemed to be thinking, I was never dull.

Cheering in the Press Box

The performance by Notre Dame left guard Ted Horansky in the 1978 Cotton Bowl proved that you can talk people into anything if you say it loud enough and often enough.

This isn't to say that Horansky needed an advertising campaign. Oh, no. His performance spoke for itself. He just needed somebody to turn up the volume and that guy was me. The problem is that offensive linemen take their cue from Teddy Roosevelt. They speak softly and carry a big stick. As a result, the skill position players get all the glory. Let's hear it for the guys in the trenches occasionally.

The 1977 national championship was decided in the Cotton Bowl which was played on Monday, Jan. 2, 1978, in deference to the pro football playoffs. Notre Dame was matched against a familiar opponent, the number one ranked Texas Longhorns, the only unbeaten team left in college football. Led by the great running back Earl Campbell, Texas was a comfortable favorite over Notre Dame, which was ranked fifth with one loss. The Irish lost their second game of the season to Ole Miss, 20-13, in Jackson, Miss.

In the days before the game, I met Ted Horansky's family in the lobby of our Dallas hotel. They were from Cleveland, so we had much in common. Ted went to Cathedral Latin. So by game time, I was looking for him, number 68, and there was a lot to see.

Notre Dame shocked the Longhorns, 38-10, and surged all the way to number one in the final rankings. The Irish scored four touchdowns on running plays, two by Terry Eurick and two by Vagas Ferguson, who also caught a touchdown pass from Joe Montana. Ferguson and Jerome Heavens rushed for over 100 yards while Campbell barely gained 100 for Texas. Both Notre Dame's offensive and defensive lines totally dominated the Longhorns.

All four rushing touchdowns came behind the left side of the line and from the press box it appeared that Horansky had a lot to do with that. Notre Dame scored three touchdowns in the second quarter, two by Eurick

After Eurick's first touchdown, a six-yard run, I remarked to no one in particular but to everyone in general, "Nice block by left guard Horansky on that touchdown."

That's not a conversation starter. You don't expect a response. I was just planting a seed, not even imagining I was fertilizing a mighty oak.

Eurick's second touchdown also was a running play to the left, ten yards. There was Horansky congratulating Eurick again.

"Big block by Horansky again," I said, a little louder. "He had the key block on both touchdowns."

Nobody said anything. Not even a "harrumph."

Ferguson ran for touchdowns in the third and fourth quarter and by then I was selling hard.

"What a block by left guard Horansky!" I bellowed in the third quarter when Ferguson bulled his way three yards into the end zone.

On Ferguson's 26-yard touchdown run in the fourth quarter, I was a raving madman. You might have thought Horansky hoisted Ferguson on his back and carried him all the way.

"Left guard Horansky had the big block on four touchdowns. What a game by Horansky!'

In the press box, it is a time-honored tradition to give nobody credit for an astute observation. You don't want to tip your hand in case you use the observation yourself. But those things tend to sink in. When it comes to line play, hardly anybody in the press box knows what is going on, so when you hear a name, you file that information away.

With five minutes left in the game, they collected the ballots for most valuable player and almost everybody checked their rosters for the spelling of Horansky. Heard his name a lot in the press box, they thought quietly to themselves. Nobody wanted to be the idiot who left him off their ballot.

The obvious people got votes. Notre Dame running backs Heavens, Ferguson and Eurick, of course, and quarterback Montana and middle linebacker Bob Golic, who helped contain Earl Campbell. Campbell also got some mentions. All the Texas reporters voted for him.

But a left guard? Yes, Horansky finished fifth in MVP voting. In that cast of All-Americans, the guy with the lunch pail almost walked off with the gold ring.

Many years later Horansky recalled an incident in the locker room after the game.

"A guy came up to me at my locker. He introduced himself. He said he was from *The New York Times*. He said he just wanted to tell me that he voted for me for most valuable player."

He must have been an astute reporter with very good hearing.

Barry Clemens: Old School

Barry Clemens, who played with the Cavs in the 1970s, said he did not want to begin his story at the beginning. No, he said he wanted to begin in the present and work backwards.

"You make the rules," I said. "I'm in your house. Your wife is making my lunch. Without you, this chapter doesn't exist."

He began the night of the Cavs-Lakers game earlier that week in January 2010. He and Elmore Smith, another NBA veteran of the 1970s whose last three years were with the Cavs, are part of their alumni association who meet and greet fans before the games in a fancy restaurant on loge level at Quicken Loans Arena.

"Dan Gilbert gives us two tickets to the games. We shake a few hands. We have dinner. And he even gives us a stipend. I'd be there anyway. I usually bring a client," said Clemens, who is now a Wells Fargo financial consultant.

"Elmore has a barbeque sauce," Clemens continued. "The Cavs use it in their restaurant. Elmore is a nice guy. He's hooked up. One thing leads to another. He introduced me to the chef, who was a scholarship football player at Michigan. I asked him what time he got there in the morning. He said seven o'clock.

"I said, 'What? Seven o'clock!' He said the players come here at 8:30 to eat breakfast before their shooting practice.

"Then they go home? 'No. After shooting practice we feed them lunch,' the chef said. 'Then they go home but before they leave they fill out a list for their post-game meal.'

"What? 'Yeah, after the game we make them a take-home dinner,' the chef said.

"I was shocked at how well they're taken care of," said Clemens.

When the Cavs are on the road and their personal chef isn't there to satisfy their every need, they must survive on $120 a day meal money. Keep in mind, these are big guys with big furnaces that require a lot of fuel.

"Now we go back to my day," said Clemens. "We got seven dollars a day meal money in 1965. We flew commercial planes. We would swap food on the plane. Some guys would swap their meat for another guy's salad."

Let's not forget, however, that airline food was haute cuisine in the 1960s, often featuring filet mignon, potato, beans, roll, butter and salad. And that was in coach. Of course, up and down the East Coast it was not unusual to travel by train or bus. Not only did they not get steak, sometimes they did not get heat.

Besides all of these amenities, Clemens made $10,000 as a rookie with the New York Knicks. Today, some guys spend that much in one night entertaining friends in a fancy restaurant.

"Pro basketball has come a long way," said Clemens, who sat back and stretched his 6-foot-7-inch frame.

Clemens grew up on a working farm in Xenia, which is in southwest Ohio near Dayton. Clemens' father, who worked the farm, had a parallel life. He was a physicist at Wright-Patterson Air Force Base a few miles away. Either he did physics on the side or he did farming on the side, but he managed to cram both careers into one life. Obviously, there were some brains in that family and Barry, one of three sons, inherited well. He breezed through school with straight A's until his senior year at Xenia High School.

"I asked one teacher as a favor to give me a B," he recalled. "I needed a B."

"But you're already getting an A," said the teacher.

"That's the problem," he told her. "If you give me an A, I'll be class valedictorian and I'll have to make a speech at graduation. I do not want the pressure of a speech."

She understood. As a favor, she lowered his grade to a B. He was not valedictorian and he did not have to make the speech.

Barry had a speech impediment. He stuttered. Over the decades, he conquered the stutter and his confidence increased. Now he's an engaging public speaker but for a 17-year-old high school senior the specter of speaking in public with a stutter was traumatic. He even called himself John because it was easier to say than Barry.

All this became a metaphor for his basketball career. Clemens was always overcoming something. For example, he went to Ohio Wesleyan University, a Division III college in Delaware, a mere 17 miles north of mighty Ohio State but in the world of college sports they were light years apart. Nevertheless, Clemens was invited to the

1964 Olympic basketball trials in St. Louis. (He was calling himself Barry by then.)

"At practice, a guy kept saying, 'Good job, Barry.' He was one of the coaches. I thought he was talking to me. It turned out he was talking to the guy I was guarding, a guy named Rick Barry. I thought I did a pretty good job guarding him."

As primitive as pro scouting was in those days, the NBA actually discovered him in those 1,000-seat gymnasiums in the Ohio Conference.

"There were pro scouts at those games. You could tell who they were. They sat alone with a clipboard. I was told that I might be drafted by the St. Louis Hawks. They sent a scout to see me play and he gave a bad report on me. Do you know who the scout was? They sent a hurt player. He wasn't playing so they thought they'd give him something to do. He was a forward and I was a forward. He wasn't going to give a good report on somebody who might take his job."

The New York Knicks drafted him in 1965 with the 19th pick in the entire draft. He was, however, the fifth player selected by the Knicks, who had bonus picks and territorial picks. Clemens was at a crossroads. He had been accepted to both dental school and optometry school.

Clemens recalls thinking, "Know your limitations," six years before Clint Eastwood actually said those words in "Dirty Harry." Basketball, he concluded, had fewer limitations. After all, he had gone nose to nose with Rick Barry and held his own.

The Knicks' rookie camp was crowded.

"They lined up 50 guys in a huge armory. I had never seen so many seven footers. There were eight of them. The next day, 30 players were cut. Eventually, only six rookies were invited to the start of training camp at Fairfield University and here's the odd part. One of the other six was Bill Meyer from Hiram College. There were two Ohio Conference guys among the final six rookies."

Only one of them made the team and that was Clemens. He recalls living in the Paramount Hotel with some of the other young, unmarried players. It's a classy place today, but in those days it was a half a notch above seedy. There was a burlesque house on the top floor and some of the strippers lived in the hotel.

"After about six or seven weeks I was called into the treasurer's office," Clemens said. "He said he had to balance the books and he wanted to know why I wasn't cashing my pay checks. 'Where are they?' he wanted to know. I had six or seven checks uncashed in the dresser under my underwear. I didn't know what to do with them. I had never had a checking account."

How did he get by in New York with no money?

"I had a few dollars but I didn't spend much. For practice we took a subway to a YMCA on 92nd Street or to an armory in New Jersey. Maybe we switched to a bus to get to New Jersey."

For a rookie, the NBA was a no frills league. Even for the veterans it was a humble life. Players often washed their own uniforms. When Clemens played for the Chicago Bulls, their white home uniforms were pink by the end of the season.

"The wives would wash our uniforms and throw our home whites in with red stuff," he said.

"One time we got to a city early on game day and we checked into a hotel but they told us not to pull back the covers. Just lay on top of the bed. We weren't going to sleep there overnight. They didn't charge us the full rate if we didn't muss up the bed."

The Cincinnati Royals were a nomadic team in the '60s. They played home games in Cleveland and Dayton, wherever a promoter guaranteed them more money than they would make at home. Later they moved to Kansas City and split time in Omaha and now they're in Sacramento.

"We played the Cincinnati Royals at the University of Dayton," Clemens said. "In the morning we flew into the Dayton airport at Vandalia and rented cars. I brought the whole team to our farm in Xenia. My mom put out a spread. She cooked steaks. Some guys rode horses. Dick Barnett did. We had 10 horses on the farm. Willis Reed brought his shotgun. He brought it on the plane. He shot skeet that afternoon. I thought I knew the way from Xenia to the University of Dayton. We told the guys to follow me. Well, I got lost. We got there late. The game was supposed to start at seven o'clock. We got there at twenty after seven."

In the NBA at that time, people rolled with the punches. Knicks coach Dick McGuire didn't let it ruin his day.

"He played me the entire second and fourth quarters because all my family and friends were there," Clemens said. "As usual, we lost by 20."

In the 1960s it seemed the entire league smoked cigarettes and drank beer. Boston Celtics coach Red Auerbach was even famous for lighting cigars on the bench at the end of games.

"We had about five guys on the team who smoked before games, they smoked at halftime and they smoked after games. The fans smoked during games. There were doubleheaders at Madison Square Garden in those days and by the middle of the second game you couldn't read the scoreboard because of the blue haze."

After one year with the Knicks, Clemens was claimed in the expansion draft by Chicago, where he encountered one of the league's great drinkers.

"When other guys were smoking, Erwin Mueller was drinking," Clemens said. "You had to get your ankles taped before walking in his apartment. It was ankle deep in beer bottles. We were in Milwaukee to play the Bucks. We had dinner at three o'clock in the afternoon and Mueller had three stingers. Do you know what goes into a stinger?"

How could a guy who drank three stingers *before* games survive in the NBA?

"Our coach, Johnny Kerr, had a warm spot in his heart for him," said Clemens.

Mueller, a skinny 6-8 center from the University of San Francisco, made the all-rookie team in 1967 and helped the Bulls make the playoffs, the only time a first-year expansion team did that. Kerr, who traded Mueller away and later traded to get him back, wasn't the only one who had a soft spot in his heart for him. Somehow Mueller managed to stick around the NBA for seven seasons with four teams and spent his final season of pro ball with two teams in the American Basketball Association.

When the Bulls played in Philadelphia, guard Guy Rodgers usually hung around with an old college pal from Temple. Rodgers' friend came to the games and he rode the team bus back to the hotel. Except for Rodgers, the rest of the team didn't know him very well but they enjoyed being around him.

"He would sit in the back of the bus talking with Guy and he was hilarious. It was like having a comedian on the bus with us. We'd lose by 20 but he'd have us laughing after the game. He was a lot of fun. We only saw him in Philadelphia," said Clemens. "One night I see this guy on television. I said, 'I know that guy. He's a friend of Guy Rodgers. He rode the bus with us.' He was Bill Cosby."

Clemens spent three years with the Bulls and had a stretch of several games when he played regularly and averaged 17 or 18 points.

"We were on the West Coast to play the San Francisco Warriors. The game was in San Jose but we had an off day. The players liked staying in Los Angeles so that's where we spent the off day. We practiced in the morning at nine o'clock and on the way back to the hotel I passed some outdoor courts so I stopped and played for a couple of hours. They didn't know who I was. One of the guys asked me to play that night in a league. It was a good league of ex-college players. They said one of their players wasn't going to make it that night, a guy named Joe Black who had played at Oregon or Oregon State. So I played and had a good game. They put me down in the official scorer's book as Joe Black. It was the first game of the season. Nobody knew anybody yet. After the game the scorer said, 'Hey, Joe. You didn't pay your $15 dollar entry fee.' I said I'll get you next time.

"The next morning we fly up to San Jose to play the Warriors. I picked up a copy of the *Los Angeles Times* on the way to the airport. We're on the plane and I'm reading the sports section. On one of the back pages there's a headline, 'Joe Black Scores 52 points.' Looks like I was stroking it."

That is unheard of today. A pro player never would join a pickup game on an asphalt court or even play for fun in an amateur league. If a knee blows out or a muscle tears, he would have some explaining to do. It would cost him millions of dollars.

But Clemens loved to play, whether he was getting paid or not. Not that the salaries were that impressive when he played. It was tough to squeeze a dollar out of the owners in those days.

In the 1960s, Reggie Harding came to the Pistons directly out of high school in Detroit and brought a gun to negotiate his contract. He later was killed in a drive-by shooting while sitting on his front porch.

Jack Kent Cooke, one of the greatest moguls in sports history, was an exception. When he owned the Los Angeles Lakers, he fired Elmore Smith's agent in the mid-'70s.

"You can't do that," protested Elmore. "Only I can fire my agent."

"He was doing such a lousy job for you, somebody had to fire him," said Cooke, who then sweetened Elmore's contract substantially.

Clemens' 11-year NBA career took him to New York, Chicago,

Seattle, Cleveland and Portland. Clemens always was a substitute but his longevity can be attributed to one thing. He could shoot from outside.

The Portland Trail Blazers' web site calls him the 10th best pure shooter in franchise history, tucked between Danny Ainge and Walt Williams and 14 places higher than Clyde Drexler.

Others called Clemens the best pure shooter of his era.

In 1973 the NBA conducted a "One on One Contest" for television. Clemens defeated four of the best shooters in the league before finally losing to Geoff Petrie in the final.

Clemens had moments when he twinkled, but he never was a star and he hungered for that. He always wanted to be Joe Black in real life.

He played in YMCA leagues and rec leagues in Cleveland until he was well into his fifties. He was once called "the best 51-year-old player on the planet."

"I always wanted to dominate a game. I would tell my wife I was going to the hardware store so I could sneak out and play," he said when he was inducted into the Greater Cleveland Sports Hall of Fame in 2009. "She thought I spent a lot of time at the hardware store."

He paid a high price for his deception. At age 50 he had a hip replacement. When he was 63 he underwent back surgery. Two stainless steel rods were inserted in his back, each a foot long, as well as 18 two-inch screws. At age 65 they went back into that hip and did some more repair work.

When he was 66 I asked him if he were ready to retire. He said he was not prepared to make such an announcement.

Larry Weiser's Season Tickets

When Larry Weiser graduated from law school in the summer of 1971 he indulged himself. He bought season tickets to the Cavs' games. Plenty of good seats were available. The previous year their average home attendance was 3,518.

"I called them up," Weiser said, "and Bill Fitch answered the phone."

Fitch was the head coach and he also was the only person working in the office that day.

"Come on down and pick out your seat," said Fitch.

The next day Fitch personally escorted Weiser around the old Cleveland Arena and helped him pick out his two seats. At that time the Cavs were the typical mom and pop store. Sometimes Fitch felt like both mom and pop.

The years passed. Fitch moved on. Players came and went. New owners bought and sold the team. Undaunted, Weiser never missed a season. When he underwent open heart surgery in 2009, the Cavs' players made a video and presented it to him. Almost every player appeared in it, urging him to "get well and cheer us on."

He showed me his exotic wine cellar and the rare bottle of wine he said he is saving for a special occasion.

"It's worth $1,000," he said. "I'll open it when the Cavs win the NBA championship."

He invited me to join him and I cleared my calendar for the entire month of June, 2010.

If wine gets better with age, I'm afraid it will be a $10,000 bottle when he finally uncorks it.

Call Him Lucky

I learned more about world history at soccer games than I ever absorbed in a classroom. There was a time when the game in Cleveland was played only by ethnic groups that harbored grudges dating back centuries. For instance, in the Lake Erie Soccer League, the ethnic league founded in Cleveland in the 1950s, we had the Croatians and the Serbians, historic rivals since the Stone Age. Their games often ended in riots.

"The games were played on Sunday afternoons," recalled Dr. Jim Samplinger, who played for the Cleveland Kickers, a German team. "The fans had just come from church and were dressed in their suits. When the games got tough, their coats would come off and out came the guns."

Referees were chased and sometimes assaulted during and after games, sometimes by both teams. Everybody seemed to have had a grievance.

But then referee Lucky Kramer stood up and said he was mad as hell and wasn't going to take it any longer. Lucky, who was a Cleveland policeman in real life, began packing a piece, a detective's model five-shot .38 caliber snub-nosed pistol. Naturally, it was loaded. Any team that went after Lucky had to send at least six men—five to take a bullet and the sixth to take down Lucky. After I did a story on him and his revolver, Lucky was treated with respect—for a referee, at least.

"A whistle in his hand and a gun in his pocket," Lucky recalled, quoting from the story.

Lucky was his legal name, not a nickname. It was suggested by the federal judge who presided over his naturalization ceremony.

"You have the opportunity to legally change your name at no cost," said the judge. "Maybe you would like to change it to 'Lucky' because you certainly have been lucky. You came here as an immigrant and now you have a job as a policeman. You are a lucky man."

It never was made clear how Lucky became a Cleveland policeman before he became a United States citizen but that was Lucky's story and he was sticking to it. Arguing the point with a man packing a snub-nosed .38 wasn't the smart play.

Lucky thought about his name. He was Hungarian and he had a typical Hungarian first name, Laszlo. As for his last name, Kramer, most people assume it is German, but no, his father, Szigmond Kramer, was Austro-Hungarian. He made a decision.

"Change my name to Lucky," he said to the judge.

Years later after refereeing a professional game between the Cleveland Cobras and a team from Buffalo played at Finnie Stadium in Berea, Lucky was not so lucky. He answered a knock at the door of the referees' dressing room and was confronted by an irate front office minion from the Buffalo team. Being from out of town, he was unaware of Lucky's pistol-packing ways. He reached back for something special and landed a punch squarely on Lucky's nose. The assailant was immediately overcome and turned over to the authorities, but he was released a few hours later with no charges filed because punching a referee was not felonious assault. No, punching a soccer referee was a minor misdemeanor comparable to a parking ticket.

Muhammad Ali: Boxing's Prettiest Face

Within a month of winning the heavyweight championship from Sonny Liston on Feb. 25, 1964, Muhammad Ali changed his name from Cassius Clay, which he explained was his "slave name," to his new Muslim name, and he instantly became a world figure. Until then we didn't realize how many Muslims there are in this world. There are a lot of them and Ali was their hero.

Like most white guys, I had never actually known anyone named Muhammad and I wasn't comfortable calling him by that name. We had just gotten to know him as Cassius. Today it's easy. We've known him as Muhammad for most of our lives. But in 1964 we chickened out and called him, "Champ." We'd say, "Yeah, Champ. Whattaya say, Champ. Way to go, Champ." He knew what was going on but he let it alone.

This Muslim stuff was puzzling. It was difficult for many of us white guys to understand how the Islam religion differed from the Black Muslims who were burning down the cities at that time.

"What the hell is going on here?" we wondered.

So I spent an afternoon with Ali on April 9, 1964, trying to get the answers and when it was over, I was more confused than before.

Ali was in town as a favor to Pete Rademacher, the former Olympic heavyweight champion, who was promoting a fight show at Baldwin-Wallace College. Ali appeared on the Mike Douglas television show on WKYC Channel 3 at noon and he attended the fight show that night in Ursprung Gym. In the middle Ali and I got together.

I picked up Ali at the television station after the show. Stepin Fetchit, an old black vaudeville star, also was a guest on the show and he needed a ride so we dropped him off at Public Square where he caught the Rapid Transit train to the airport. His bones creaked as he got out of the back seat of my old Ford and I noticed that Ali slipped a $100 bill into his hand.

From there it was off to the Majestic Hotel on East 55th Street, just north of Central Avenue. Ali could have stayed at any hotel— our downtown hotels in Cleveland were not segregated—but he preferred the Majestic, a 19th century mansion converted to a hotel that catered only to blacks. As we parked alongside the hotel and walked to the front entrance, children from George Washington Carver Elementary School recognized Ali from across the street. It was dismissal time and hundreds of kids suddenly appeared. These children were no more than 12 or 13 years old, but they already knew the heavyweight champion. In those days, there was only one champion and there he was in real life. I doubt that the children would have recognized Sonny Liston or Floyd Patterson, Ali's immediate predecessors as heavyweight champion, but they knew Ali, even though he had been heavyweight champion for only six weeks. That's the immediate impact he had on the world.

When Ali saw an audience, a switch in his brain clicked and it was show time. They waved and called his name. Ali called back.

"Who's the greatest?" he shouted.

"You're the greatest," they responded.

And so it went for several minutes. The kids poured onto the street, blocking traffic on a major north-south artery and for several minutes they shut down a large portion of Cleveland's East Side. Ali led the chants and the kids answered until the champion grew tired and we slipped away into the hotel.

We squeezed into a tiny elevator and rode to the fourth floor—the top floor—and retreated to his small room. Ten years later Ali traveled with an entourage of dozens and he rented entire floors of shiny new hotels. But in the spring of 1964 his only traveling companion was his road manager, a man named Archie Kariem. In the privacy of his room Ali exhaled loudly and his tall body seemed to slump. The show was over.

"It's an act," he said.

"What's an act?" I said. "Your act with the kids out there? Your act with Sonny Liston before the fight?"

His entire public life, he said, was a performance. It was his signature. He was a promoter. His wild-eyed proclamations leading up to his fight with Sonny Liston in Miami Beach were orchestrated to generate interest and sell tickets.

"Float like a butterfly, sting like a bee," was Ali's anthem leading up to the Liston bout, but it was suspected that his obnoxious cornerman Drew (Bundini) Brown was the actual author.

At every opportunity Ali ridiculed and discredited Liston. No sport, not even boxing had ever seen anything so outrageous. Ali called Liston an ugly chump and said it was time for "a pretty face" to rule boxing. He caressed his face like a model selling cosmetics.

Until then fighters never made incendiary comments. The most quotable was Joe Louis' prophetic remark about former light heavyweight champion Billy Conn. "He can run but he can't hide," Louis said before their 1941 fight.

"I don't hate Sonny Liston. I never did," Ali said that afternoon. "I went over to his house a few days before the fight and told him exactly what I was going to do and why. Liston agreed. I have advisors telling me exactly what to do. We plan out everything I say in advance, just like the president has his cabinet. But the fight was for real."

We got to the Muslims. What were their beliefs? What were his beliefs?

Integration, he said, will not work because it is not the natural order. Blacks and whites should live in peace but separately. They should have nothing to do with each other.

We were both young, inexperienced and naïve. He was 22. I was 26. Blacks and whites alike were dying in marches and sit-ins and I thought they were noble. Ali dismissed their courage as futility. I wasn't going to fight him over our views. I wasn't there to debate him.

"I get more hell from colored folks than from white folks for being a Muslim," he said. "I don't hate anybody. I want to live in peace. I go where I'm wanted. If I'm not wanted, I move on. I don't bash in store windows. I don't march and picket. I can't carry on like that. I'm too big a man for that. You white folks are the ones who have the problem. You don't know whether to support one Negro group or the other."

Because there was no chair in the room, I sat on the edge of his bed writing down everything he said, filling up my notebook. Ali had taken off his suit coat and hung it on a hanger in his small closet and was standing in front of a mirror as he expounded on his philosophies. All the time he rubbed some type of ointment from a little blue jar on his face and hands. This went on for a long time. He continually worked it into his skin.

I couldn't see the jar because it was on top of a highboy dresser. It would have been rude to ask him what he was doing, so I stood up—as though to stretch—so I could read the label.

"Whitening cream!" That's what it said.

This day was getting crazier. While he was advocating separation of the races, he was rubbing whitening cream into his face and hands. Forty-five years later I related the story to Stacey Bell of Channel 8.

"That's not uncommon," she said. "Whitening cream is used to balance the complexion. Some persons of color have uneven pigments. Darker in some areas. Lighter in others. Whitening cream evens it all out."

This was overkill. His skin was perfectly pigmented. His entire body was exactly the same shade. There were no variations. It was obvious to millions of people who saw him in the ring wearing only boxing shorts. Everything about his skin can be explained. He had a light complexion because of an Irish grandfather, which also accounts for his boastful personality and penchant for poetry.

If I could turn back the clock to 1964, I would ignore good manners and say to Ali, "What in the hell are you doing?" But I was an invited guest in his hotel room. It was no time for confrontation. There are rules for invited guests. Good manners are involved. I just kept writing in my notebook and turning the pages.

And that's how it went over the next 15 years. Ali was responsible for some of the most thrilling events in my life. I covered his comeback victory over Jerry Quarry in Atlanta, two of his fights with Joe Frazier, his win over Ken Norton in Yankee Stadium, his survival of Earnie Shaver's relentless attack in Madison Square Garden.

Ali inflicted terrible punishment on the obscure Chuck Wepner at the Richfield Coliseum in 1975. After the fight I had to search out Wepner. I found him standing over the drain in his shower. He was dressed in a suit, dress shirt, open neck, no tie, and he was standing over the drain in his shower, convulsing with the dry heaves. Ali gave Wepner more than a beating. He gave him the biggest payday of his life in a one-sided fight that became Sylvester Stallone's inspiration for the movie franchise, *Rocky*.

Explaining Ali is impossible. He was a contradiction. What he said about blacks and whites back in 1965, I don't believe he meant a word of it. During his entire boxing career his trainer was Angelo Dundee, an Italian. His bodyguard was the big Irish lummox Gene Kilroy. Although he gave Don King credibility as a promoter, Ali also fought several times for white promoter Bob Arum. And he gave Irish sportswriters a lifetime of stories.

Don Elbaum:
He Took It on the Chin

Decades later they still don't know who blew up boxing promoter Don Elbaum's car. His 1967 Pontiac was lit up in the parking lot of the Highlander Motor Inn in Warrensville Heights at 2:30 a.m. on Jan. 20, 1972. Elbaum was tucked away in his room when somebody placed four sticks of dynamite in a front wheel well and lit a simple fuse.

"It wasn't that good a job," Elbaum told me. "It only destroyed the front end of the car. It's now a Gremlin. It needed an oil change, anyway. What makes me mad is I just put a new battery in it."

"It definitely was a warning," said Warrensville Heights police chief Herbert E. Burgess.

Within a few years Cleveland was known as the car bomb capital of the world. We were blowing up a dozen cars a year, sometimes with people in them. The most famous, of course, were gangsters Alex (Shondor) Birns and Danny Greene. Birns was blown up when he started his Cadillac behind a striptease joint on Detroit Avenue and West 25th Street. Pieces of him were scattered around the neighborhood and it was said that a testicle landed on the front steps of nearby St. Malachi's Church. Greene was blown up to avenge Shondor's death. Greene was vaporized in the parking lot of his dentist's office at Brainard Road and Cedar Road in Mayfield Heights. A molar landed on the Cedar Road entrance ramp to I-271. So much for painless dentistry.

"Elbaum ought to be careful," said Warrensville Heights Detective John Kalavsky. "He should get a bodyguard."

"That's not true," said Elbaum. "What I need is a chauffeur."

When the police asked Elbaum for a list of possible suspects or a motive, he said, "You'll need a bigger notebook. It could have been anybody."

"Do you owe anybody any money?" the detective asked.

"How much time to do you have?" said Elbaum. "I owe everybody."

Sure he owed money. After every fight, his creditors and silent partners lined up like the second shift at Republic Steel on payday. But nobody threatened him, in person or over the phone. Elbaum was such a likable and well-intentioned fellow that many people had no problem loaning him money with no expectation of getting paid back. If it was a warning, somebody should have told him what he was being warned about.

When boxing promoter Larry Atkins retired in 1964 after promoting the second Joey Giardello-Rocky Rivero fight at the old Cleveland Arena, the Cleveland fight game was engulfed in a vacuum and if there's anything that appealed to Don Elbaum, it was a vacuum. In he swept like a high pressure system. Elbaum was in his mid-30s when he came to Cleveland to promote professional boxing. He was young, energetic and idealistic. He had promoted fights in his hometown of Erie, Pa., and in Akron. Cleveland was a bigger market and it had the 10,000-seat Cleveland Arena. Elbaum dreamed of filling it with fisticuffs.

He never came close. At one time Cleveland was one of the boxing capitals of the country. There were New York, Chicago and Cleveland. The first event in Cleveland Stadium was a heavyweight championship fight, July 3, 1931, Max Schmeling vs. Young Stribling. But when Elbaum arrived in 1968, the fight game in Cleveland was almost dead. Every promotion was a struggle. Elbaum brought in some decent fighters over the years—among them George Foreman, Ken Norton, Floyd Patterson, Emile Griffith, Don Fullmer—either before they were famous or when they were on their way out. Every show was a financial adventure. He usually involved partners, investors, who enjoyed the thrill of the fight game and the emotional high that comes with first row ringside.

Elbaum was not an accountant, but he had a knack for creative bookkeeping. For example, he owned the contracts of two promising welterweights, Frankie Kolovrat of Cleveland and Arthur (Tap) Harris of Akron. It has never been legal for promoters to own fighters, but the rule was loosely, if ever, enforced. In boxing, only the ring is square. All the other corners are rounded. Elbaum built up their records against carefully picked opponents for a showdown on April 26, 1972, at the Arena.

Both were unbeaten, according to their published records, although Elbaum concealed the fact that Kolovrat's winning streak had ended 13 days earlier when he fought in Las Vegas under the name Frankie Kolo. Never allow a minor discrepancy to mar the big picture, Elbaum always reasoned.

At five o'clock on the day of the battle of unbeatens, Elbaum checked the advance sale at the Arena box office. It was not good.

"I'm going to sell your contract," Elbaum told Kolovrat.

That's exactly what he did. He sold Kolovrat's contract to Kolovrat that very night.

"As I recall," Elbaum told me later, "the selling price happened to be exactly what Kolovrat's purse was that night."

That was a bad deal for Kolovrat. When he bought himself, he bought a wild free swinger with no boxing skills. The skillful and athletic Harris threw a 10-round shutout at Kolovrat and Fabulous Frankie, the Croatian windmill, went on to drop 13 of 17 fights until the Ring Record Book lost track of him. Frankie had the heart of a lion but the dexterity of a hippopotamus.

A special relationship existed among Elbaum, Harris and another Akron fighter, middleweight contender Doyle Baird. They made up the Three Musketeers of boxing. Sadly, just as Harris cracked the world top 10 and was headed for big money, he had the bad luck to kill a guy and went to the Mansfield Reformatory for six years. No one argued about the nobility of the crime. The man had threatened Tap's mother and, as everyone knew, when you threaten someone's mother in Akron, that is the last mother you will threaten. That is probably why Tap served only six years.

Don, Doyle and I visited Tap in prison. Doyle said it was like going back for his junior high school reunion because he had served time in the same institution for manslaughter. While in prison Doyle showed his toughness and learned to box. I won't say it was a pleasant visit, with steel bars in front of us and steel doors slamming behind us. We were surrounded by guys with long faces and unhappy eyes. That is where they shot the movie, *The Shawshank Redemption*. As we were leaving, Tap Harris suggested that we leave Elbaum behind because he had been getting away with murder for years.

Nobody made much money fighting for Elbaum, but the memories are forever. John Griffin, a tough Cleveland light heavyweight, fought for Elbaum often enough that he worked around that situation. On the night of June 30, 1971, Griffin spotted 70 pounds to the big, lumbering heavyweight from Philadelphia, Jack O'Halloran, and pounded him at will for 10 rounds. If O'Halloran had any sense, he would have looked for a soft spot on the canvas. This is the same Jack O'Halloran who later moved to Hollywood to make movies. He was a big palooka who occasionally had some speaking lines, much like his boxing career.

After the fight, Griffin sent two ladies of the night to O'Halloran's room in the old Versailles Hotel on Euclid Avenue to comfort him and tend to his wounds. As O'Halloran was pre-occupied with one of these compassionate ladies, the other one dropped O'Halloran's purse out the window to Griffin, who was waiting below.

Don Elbaum brightened my life. We traveled to Muhammad Ali's training camps together. We traveled to fight shows in other cities, never in his car. He cemented our friendship by giving me a pair of boxing gloves.

"These gloves were worn by Sugar Ray Robinson in his last fight, Nov. 10, 1965, in Pittsburgh. I promoted that fight. He gave them to me and now I'm giving them to you as a sign of our friendship," Elbaum said. It was an emotional moment. I shook his hand vigorously and I hugged him.

Later, I was in a bar in Akron. Displayed on the wall in an honored position above the cash register was a pair of tattered boxing gloves.

"Those are the gloves worn by Sugar Ray Robinson in his last fight," the bartender said.

He said he bought them at an auction for $100. The auctioneer was Don Elbaum.

I sensed one night that he would have trouble paying his fighters. The pre-sale was weak and there was no walk-up. I stuck $700 in my pocket and slipped it to him. He needed it and he took it. I knew I would get it back, but never knew how or when. It took years and I never lost faith. He just had to figure out a way.

A few years later Don put together an investment group to televise a fight show from the Cincinnati Gardens. For his ringside announcers, he turned to two old friends—yours truly and Karolyn Rose, the wife of Pete Rose. I was paid $700. I don't know what he paid Karolyn. It probably depended on how much he owed her. On the books, Karolyn and I were expenses and we came off the top, before the profits were distributed to the investors.

Not long afterward Don secured the state of Ohio closed circuit rights for the huge Duran-Sugar Ray Leonard fight on June 20, 1980. For this fight he wanted to rent the Stadium. He met with Dino Lucarelli, who handled bookings for the Stadium Corp. Let's pick up my column of May 12, 1980.

* * *

"It's going to be an unbelievable, colossal fight, a phenomenal money-maker, the greatest athletic event we have seen so far in this decade," Elbaum promised.

"Whew," said Lucarelli. "I don't know if the Stadium is big enough to handle it."

"Actually," said Elbaum, "I only need about 10,000 seats."

Lucarelli checked his book. June 20 was available. The Indians were on the road.

"As I understand it," said Lucarelli, "you want to put up a big television screen in the middle of the infield."

Elbaum said that was correct.

"Will people be able to see the picture on the screen in broad daylight?" Lucarelli asked.

"Of course not," said Elbaum. "The fight is at night."

"June 20," said Lucarelli, "is the day before the longest day of the year. The sun won't go down until about a quarter to 10 that night."

"Boy, am I lucky," said Elbaum.

Lucarelli looked dumbfounded.

"I'm lucky I didn't rent the ballpark in Anchorage, Alaska," said Elbaum. "Up there the sun won't go down until October."

He has another minor problem with a fight show he's putting on this Saturday night in Dayton, completely unrelated to the Duran-Leonard mega-spectacle.

The names of the main event combatants—Tom Fischer of Dayton and Lupe Guerra of Omaha—are virtually unknown in the civilized sporting world and for good reason. They are a couple of bums.

"They've both fought nobody but stiffs," said Elbaum, "which is why they have sensational records. Fischer is 31-4 and Guerra is 14-0."

The problem is that Guerra's manager takes his fighter seriously and is worried that he could lose a hometown decision to the local boy. To minimize such a risk, Guerra's manager is insisting on neutral judges—a white, a black and a Mexican-American—all from out of town.

Elbaum proposed a less expensive option.

"We'll get three sportswriters to judge the fight," said Elbaum. "One from a big paper, one from a small paper, and one from a medium-sized paper."

He nominated me from the big papers.

"Don't they have a boxing commission in Dayton?" I asked.

Elbaum said they did.

"Who are they?" I demanded.

"You're talking to him," Elbaum replied.

"What do they pay for judging fights down there?" I inquired.

"Fifteen dollars," said Elbaum. "But the license costs $20. You owe me five."

The Indy 500:
Years of Fire and Rain

I'm still drawn to the Indianapolis 500. It's always run on Memorial Day weekend, which is the first big weekend for our family at the summer place at the lake.

"As usual, Dad's not here," Maddy complains. "He's at home watching the Indianapolis 500 on television."

I'm mesmerized by the entire pageant—the release of the balloons, the moment of silence and, best of all, native son Jim Nabors singing, "Back Home Again in Indiana." We are anchored by these traditions, such as "My Old Kentucky Home" at the Kentucky Derby, "New York, New York" at the Belmont Stakes and "Script Ohio" at the Horseshoe. If you want to make me cranky, start jabbering when the Notre Dame band plays the alma mater at a football game or when the organist plays "Ave Maria" at a wedding. These are times to shut the hell up.

The Indianapolis 500 and I go way back. When I was a kid, it was shrouded in legend and mystique. This was long before television. Fox Movietone News showed 60 seconds of the race in the movie theaters from 1927 through 1963. The newsreels would show the start, a couple of crashes, the checkered flag and the winner guzzling milk from a glass quart bottle. The script was usually cute and syrupy, except when somebody got killed, which was fairly often.

The newspapers would usually run a picture the next day. I still remember a shot in the 1950s of flaming gasoline stretching entirely across the track and cars diving down onto the grass to get by, which gives you an idea about racing at the Indianapolis Motor Speedway. The guys who drove there were daredevils. I had to see it for myself and meet these guys.

And so I covered 16 of them beginning in 1965 and before long I felt like Ernie Pyle, the war correspondent. At Indianapolis racing was not fun and games. The most important statistic was the body count. Jim Murray of the *Los Angeles Times* began one column, "Gentlemen, start your coffins."

By 1973 the Indianapolis 500 was out of control. Every year the Speedway would build more bleachers and get a new ambulance, but very little thought and few dollars went into making the race safer. A quarter of a million people filwled the bleachers and most of them were there to see cars crash. The purists have always howled that this is a cheap, inaccurate characterization. Let them scream. They are drowned out by the wails of the ambulance sirens.

Here's a "wow" statistic. In the first 57 races climaxing with the chaotic 1973 edition, the Indianapolis 500 averaged exactly one kill a year. Fifty-seven races, 57 dead. The carnage included drivers, crewmen, track workers and spectators. To clarify and explain, these numbers include practice and qualifying as well as race day. Essentially, we're talking about the entire month of May.

I was sucked in, like a rubber necker slowing down to watch the remains of a car wreck, and I think most of us in the mainstream sports media at the time would say the same thing. The guys from *Autoweek* talked about cam shafts, cubic inches, rpm's and horsepower. I envisioned cars doing fiery cartwheels down the main straightaway.

The herding instinct was a magnetic force at Indianapolis. The technical guys, speaking their unique language, hung around with each other. The football, baseball and boxing guys, off on a weekend sabbatical from the ballparks, gravitated to each other. We were in the discovery phase of our coverage.

One year I asked Mario Andretti about his race strategy.

"I'm gonna stand on it," said Mario.

That was technical enough for me. I went with it.

I spotted Leigh Montville of the *Boston Globe* walking out of A.J. Foyt's garage in Gasoline Alley.

"What'd he say?" I asked.

"He said come back in an hour," said Montville.

"Do you think he'll really be there in an hour?" I asked.

"No," said Montville. "He said the same thing yesterday."

* * *

The first auto race I ever saw was the one I covered in 1965 at the Indianapolis Motor Speedway. *The Plain Dealer* had never covered an auto race before, except for midget racers at the Stadium. It was a breakthrough year on many fronts. Scotsman Jimmy Clark was the first foreigner since Frenchman Gaston Chevrolet in 1920 to win the 500. Clark's green racer was the first rear-engine machine to win and the first to eclipse 150 miles per hour. No front engine car ever won at Indianapolis again. Colin Chapman was the first English car builder to win and his Lotus was the first English chassis. The times, they were a-changing. The only thing American about the winner's circle was the eight-cylinder Ford engine tucked in behind the driver.

The next year, 1966, the month of May did not begin well. Driver Chuck Rodee crashed in practice and was killed. That left 77 cars trying to qualify for 33 spots in the starting field.

Our racing consultant, Jeff Scott, the purest of the pure, told me that the only way to really enjoy the race was to cover it from the pits. That was an insane idea, but I didn't know that. So there I was in the pits, with 300 gallons of methanol in above-ground storage tanks every 30 feet and before half the field reached the starting line the place started to go crazy.

Starter Pat Vidan waved the green flag and 33 cars accelerated from 120 miles an hour to 200 miles an hour in about half a second. As the roar of the engines washed over me there was a cloud of dust in the vicinity of the starting line. Then there was smoke, the engines became silent, the crowd uttered an audible gasp. All I could see through the smoke was A.J. Foyt climbing the wire mesh restraining screen with flames nipping at the seat of his pants. It was the biggest crash in Indy history. Sixteen cars were involved, almost half the starting lineup. Eleven could not be repaired and were out of the race before they reached the starting line. Five were fixed in the pits and returned to racing when it was re-started after an hour and 18 minutes. Miraculously, no one was hurt. Another foreigner, Graham Hill of England, was the winner.

* * *

Two years later, 1968, Mike Spence was killed in a practice crash and Bob Hurt was paralyzed from the neck down in a particularly violent accident while trying to qualify.

Hurt, a former high school high jumper and basketball player at the University of Illinois, had been trying to qualify at Indianapolis since 1964 but never made the race. In 1975 he returned to Indianapolis for the first time since that cruel day that changed his life. This time his ride was a wheelchair.

I knew he was a former racer. At Indianapolis you saw men walking around with only one arm. You saw men with permanent limps. You saw men with their facial features burned away. Bob Hurt was in a wheelchair and a nurse was pushing him around. The Indianapolis Speedway did everything to him but kill him. It broke every bone in his body and paralyzed him but it didn't break his spirit.

"This is probably the meanest racetrack in the world," he said. "It has made a lot of people and it has broken a lot of people. No one ever got in a race car thinking he was gonna be injured. If I could, I'd get in one tomorrow. But I don't know if I would feel comfortable mentally going fast. And if you don't go fast, you're out of business.

"I have no regrets," he said as his nurse wiped his brow. "No one forced me to race. No one put a gun to my head and said, 'Get in that car.' Racing is a calculated risk. I hold no grudge in any way. This is my butt that's in this wheelchair and I'm the only one who can get it out."

He reflected on that fateful moment when he attempted to qualify on the final day in a car he had never driven.

"Because of all the rain, there was no rubber on the track," he said. "You need rubber to give you adhesion. I always had second thoughts about jumping into a strange car. I got skinned up once before doing that. Nothing serious. I broke a couple of arms. But the pressure was on. And when the pressure is on, you try to run as hard as you can in a strange car."

He went into the first turn frontways and came out of it backwards.

"I couldn't have hit the wall more square if I had taken a plumb and lined it up. I hit the wall backwards at 180 miles an hour. My body became fused with the engine. I was stunned but I was conscious.

"When I finally stopped down around turn two, I looked around to see if it was on fire and it was, but the safety crew was on me in seconds and had the fire out. I tried to move my right hand to release my safety belt and I couldn't move it. 'Doggone,' I said. 'My arm's broken.'

"I tried to move my left hand. I couldn't. 'Doggone,' I said again. 'It's broken, too. Now I'm going to miss Milwaukee.' About then I realized I couldn't breathe. My esophagus was pushed against my trachea."

When they got him to Methodist Hospital near the Speedway, which does a brisk business every May, they discovered almost every bone in his body was broken at least once. His right shoulder was shattered in three places. His left shoulder was broken in two places. His arms, legs, hands, fingers and ribs were broken. His feet were crushed. His spinal cord was crushed, high, near his neck, but it wasn't severed. His stomach and intestines were ripped away from their moorings and he was bleeding internally.

For three years he lay flat on his back, able to move only his eyeballs and his head. His savings were exhausted. He and his wife divorced by mutual consent. His family life in a comfortable home in Potomac, Maryland, where his three daughters learned to ride horses, was only a memory.

"Race car drivers are pretty hard to insure," he said.

Nevertheless, Hurt underwent 16 operations thanks to the United States Auto Club, the governing body of Indy car racing at the time, which dipped into its Benevolent Fund. His greatest triumph was the day he flicked a fly off his hand. It was the first voluntary reaction by an extremity. By the time we talked in 1975, he could shrug his shoulders and raise his arms, but his hands remained useless.

"You don't know what it meant to be able to touch an itch on my nose," he said. "Now I'm starting to feel a little pain and I love it. If I feel pain, it means I can feel."

For 32 years he never quit searching for a cure and he encouraged others to do the same. Actor Christopher Reeve was among many whom Hurt called to offer advice and hope. Hurt, however, never walked and he died in a Toronto, Canada, hotel room on Sept. 23, 2000, of prostate cancer.

*   *   *

Drivers were not the only ones who crashed. The Indianapolis Motor Speedway sometimes went out of its way to flirt with danger. In 1971 they turned over the pace car to Eldon Palmer, who owned a big

Dodge dealership in Indianapolis. Palmer provided dozens of Dodge Challengers for use in the various 500 festival events that year and his reward was to drive the pace car.

This job was not entirely ceremonial. Palmer had an important function. He set the pace for the start. He led the field around the track at 120 miles per hour during the parade lap and pace lap. Starter Pat Vidan took his cue to wave the green flag when Palmer peeled off into the pits.

Palmer drove perfectly. He sent the field off on a clean start. But he forgot one thing. He forgot to stop. He roared through the pits and never slowed down, finally skidding sideways into a crowded photographers' stand at the end of pit row. Twenty people were thrown off the raised stand and were injured, including a doctor from South America who was never the same. Palmer's passengers in the car were not injured. They were astronaut John Glenn, Speedway owner Tony Hulman and a sportscaster.

The following year a practice crash claimed the life of driver Jim Malloy, which was a preamble to the next year's race that saw the worst outbreak of fire and carnage in the storied Speedway's history. Even I was revolted. It was time for drastic changes. The world's sporting press demanded accountability.

In May 1973 Art Pollard was killed in a practice crash and then the racing gods became really angry.

An 11-car crash at the start of the race sent debris flying over the safety screen and into the stands. Eleven spectators were injured, nine were hospitalized. In the crash, driver Salt Walther's car was split in half and his legs were sticking out of the shell near the starting line. It caught fire and he was burned over 40 percent of his body. Both his knees were crushed. His ribs were broken. So were his left ankle and left wrist. One hand was burned off. When I saw him two years later he was wearing a black leather glove where his left hand had been.

"I was wearing my fire suit," he recalled. "The suit protects you for 38 seconds. I was upside down in that car for six minutes. Do you know what your skin does in a fire? It blisters like bacon sizzling in a frying pan."

Walther said he looked at movies of that crash a hundred times.

"I know why it happened," he said. "Somebody hit me from behind. One of two guys. I think I know who but it isn't important to place the blame. If that happened out on the street, you'd sue somebody. You don't do that at Indianapolis."

It began to rain before the race could be restarted and it rained for two days. On the third day the race resumed only to be cursed by more pain and rain. On lap 57, California driver Swede Savage, who had been one of the early race leaders, pulled out of the pits with a full load of fuel and sped off to eternity. He was running in third place. But he crashed coming out of turn four and came to rest on the outside wall at the top of the main straightaway. Savage's car caught fire. His ruptured fuel tanks gushed flaming methanol all over the cockpit.

From the overhanging press box above the start-finish line, I looked at Savage's car through binoculars. "It's taking the fire trucks a long time to get there," I thought. Seconds went by and then a minute or two and all the time Savage was still inside his burning racer. He hadn't moved. I was getting nervous and I was fidgeting. I was watching a man burn to death and I couldn't help. I was in the second deck, 1,000 feet away. No one was doing anything. I put down my binoculars and looked around for the fire engines. Then, directly in front of me I saw a fire truck racing through the pits the wrong way. Normally pit row is a one-way street but the fire engine had no choice. It couldn't go up the main straightaway dodging oncoming race cars. I saw a man running down the middle of pit lane and I saw the fire truck hit him from behind. He never saw it coming. He flew into the air like a rag doll and landed 50 feet away.

The man was Armando Teran, a crewman for the second car on Savage's race team, which made him part of Swede's racing family. His instincts took over and he was desperately running to rescue his friend. What was he going to do when he got to the wreck, fight through the flames and pull Savage out of the car with his bare hands? Probably, but none of that mattered. Teran was dead on arrival at the track hospital.

Savage lingered in agony for 35 days until he died July 2 at the University of Michigan burn unit.

The rains came again and the race was mercifully halted after 133 laps, Gordon Johncock the winner.

No racetrack in the world killed them like Indianapolis and the world finally demanded, "Enough!" Hulman had to act. His advisors told him the logical starting point was chief steward Harlan Fengler, an unfriendly, arrogant man. He was responsible for getting 33 cars around the Speedway 200 times and getting them home safely and he did a lousy job. From 1958 until he was relieved of duty after the 1973 race, he witnessed 15 deaths in 15 years, including 11 drivers, and he showed neither concern nor remorse.

An Indianapolis banker named Tom Binford was appointed chief steward after the 1973 debacle and the body count plummeted. Under Binford, the attitude changed.

Swede Savage was the last driver to die from injuries in the Indianapolis 500. Since then only three drivers have been killed, all in practice crashes. A fourth driver died during tire testing for Firestone. One spectator succumbed during the race.

* * *

None of the foregoing dissuaded me from a lifelong ambition. I wanted to drive around the Indianapolis Motor Speedway and I got my chance in the spring of 1967.

While suffering from a case of temporary insanity, I bought a brand new, right-off-the-boat burgundy Jaguar, the classic two-passenger XKE roadster with a speedometer that went up to 160 miles per hour. It was possibly the most beautiful car ever made and mechanically it was the worst. It was the English way of getting even for tossing their tea into Boston Harbor.

Jim Cook, head of Firestone's racing division, arranged for me to drive it around the Speedway when Firestone was using the track for tire testing. He had a racing suit waiting for me and introduced me to drivers Mario Andretti, Joe Leonard and Lloyd Ruby, who were under contract to Firestone.

Mario jumped into the passenger seat next to me and we made our run. They turned on the timing lights and the track went green.

If I were crazy, Mario Andretti was crazier. He took a ride with a madman and he did not wear a helmet. Mario gestured to dive low into the turns but no amount of advice prepared me for coming out of the turns. Centrifugal force carried us up the banked track to the wall. My skinny street tires did not grip the pavement like wide racing tires. I wasn't driving Andy Granatelli's equipment. I was driving my own car. I backed off the accelerator before scraping the wall. I glanced at Andretti. He didn't have a worry in the world. He was ready to take a nap.

Down the straightaways, however, it was pedal to the metal. We passed skid marks on the track and crash marks on the walls. This was only two months since the race and rain had not yet washed away the evidence.

When we returned to the pits, I eagerly asked about my speed. Frankly, except for one glance at Andretti, my eyes were frozen to the road.

"One-hundred and nineteen miles an hour," I was told.

"That can't be. This car should go 160," I said.

"Not when you're dragging a parachute," said one of the mechanics.

I had neglected to tie down the convertible top with a toneau cover and it ballooned behind us like the parachute that slows down the Space Shuttle when it lands.

The top never fit properly after that and rain poured through. The car soon developed various mechanical problems. It didn't start in cold weather. It was not a winter car. Everyone agreed that the 1967 Jaguar should have been displayed on the mantel and admired but never driven. But we had our moment. We had raced the clock at Indianapolis.

* * *

In the meantime I had covered several races in Europe, including the 1967 Grand Prix of Monaco in Monte Carlo, the famous race run through the city streets and along the bay. Even this idyllic setting was tainted by the agony of death. Lorenzo Bandini, the young star of the Ferrari team, crashed on a plaza overlooking the bay. His car caught fire and he burned to death. He died that night.

Despite all the carnage, I was thrilled when I learned that the Indy car series was coming to Burke Lakefront Airport in Cleveland. I stumbled upon the story by accident in a conversation with ABC announcer Chris Economaki at the Indianapolis 500 in 1981. Because of their unique planning requirements, TV networks usually know everything first. That Sunday I broke the story that Cleveland would host an annual race beginning in 1982 on the Fourth of July weekend. I hoped that the charm of Monaco would be recreated in Cleveland.

Not a chance. Despite the best efforts of promoters Chuck Newcomb and Jim Foster, the airport venue was hot and dusty. The airport was turned into tent city for a weekend. It was more like a campground than Monte Carlo.

Furthermore, the race was boring because there were no walls to bounce off. The serpentine course was slow because of a dozen twists and turns. They had to slow down to 30 miles an hour to navigate the hairpin first turn. Cars spun out on grassy expanses and got right back in the race. There was no danger. Drivers complained that their rear ends took a beating because the runways were bumpy, but that was the worst that happened.

Nevertheless, the race lasted 26 years before the final checkered flag fluttered over the lakefront in 2007. Along the way *The Plain Dealer* forced out Newcomb and Foster with a series of complaints about their accounting practices. The race was taken over by Roger Penske, who gave way to Mark McCormack's IMG and finally Mike Lanigan of Chicago. At the end the economy soured, the two rival Indy car racing leagues merged and there was no room on the schedule for Cleveland.

* * *

Having personally chronicled much of this tableau, I readily agreed that only a lunatic would go racing.

And so, on June 15, 1996, for the purpose of doing a television story for WJW-TV, I went racing with the good old boys at Barberton Speedway. They painted a miniature stock car in WJW colors and I was entered in an eight-car race on the compact one-eighth-mile track. To drive the car it was necessary to assume a supine position with my feet forward on the gas and brake pedals.

Because we started in reverse order of our qualifying times, the slower cars in front, a concept that encourages passing, I was in first place on the first lap and I was determined no one would pass me. I took turn three too fast and lost control on the short chute between turns three and four. Suddenly the racer was upside down, skidding along on its roof backward, which put me on my stomach head first into the outside wall. I hit head on at about 40 miles an hour. My car was all one piece, which was not good. It didn't break apart like real race cars do today. It hit the wall and bounced back but my organs kept going straight. My body absorbed all the energy.

I was convinced my neck or back was broken, possibly both.

"Don't move. We'll get you out," one of the track workers said.

"Don't worry, I won't," I said.

I wasn't going to play the hero. I was afraid I was in big trouble.

Meanwhile, my wife and the four kids arrived in the Chevy station wagon and were greeted by a nervous receptionist at the pass gate who said, "You're here just in time, Mrs. Coughlin. They're putting your husband in the ambulance now."

They escorted her onto the track and she peeked in the back door of the ambulance. I know she thought I was an idiot but she tried to hide it. She pretended to be concerned.

"I'm fine," I told her. "They're just going to run me down to the hospital to make sure. I'll meet you and the kids right back here in an hour."

One lonely doctor with more than a few years on his résumé was on duty in the emergency room of Barberton Hospital. I wondered why he was still pulling Saturday night duty in the ER. But I didn't dwell on his problem. I had plenty of my own. I figured I had crushed some vertebrae and ruptured some organs. My insides were in agony. I looked ahead to a year of rehab.

Much to my surprise, none of those things had happened. I was fine in the sense that there was no permanent damage but soon another problem developed. The emergency room doctor gave me a prescription for muscle relaxers. Please, never take muscle relaxers. They don't discriminate. They find a muscle, they relax it. They even shut down the intestines, which means they shut down peristalsis. If you don't know what peristalsis is, look it up. Mine stopped working for several days. Next time I hit a wall head on, I'll take an aspirin.

Rosie Ruiz Loses in a Photo Finish

When Rosie Ruiz was the first woman across the finish line at the Boston Marathon in 1980, I was the first one to interview her.

She was an amazing woman. I marveled at her conditioning. She wasn't perspiring. She wasn't even out of breath. She told me she was from Manhattan and that she trained in Central Park during her lunch hour.

The writers who were familiar with marathon runners soon gathered around us. They were skeptical. Nobody from the New York Road Runners Club had heard of her and marathon winners usually don't come from out of nowhere.

Back in the media center I called the office in Manhattan where she said she worked.

"Does Rosie Ruiz work there?" I asked.

"Yes, she does," said the voice that answered the phone.

"What do you think about her winning the Boston Marathon?" I asked.

"She won what?!!!" said the woman in the office.

Within 48 hours, Rosie was exposed as a fraud. Reviews of videotape uncovered no trace of her along the 26-mile course. No other runners reported seeing her. No one else in the race even knew her. Evidently, Rosie had jumped off a bus and slipped into the pack near the finish line and for two days she was the women's champion. To this day, she has never explained herself. She has moved to Miami and has had a couple of scrapes with the law.

I would have figured her out if I had heard the bus tokens jingling in the pocket of her shorts.

Whispering John Duffy:
He Could Pick a Winner

Whispering John Duffy never gave anything to anybody for nothing—except on one Christmas Eve many years ago.

Duffy is long gone and I regret that I knew him only as an old man who hustled socks and underwear out of cardboard boxes in the back stairwell of an old newspaper building.

In his youth Duffy was a nightclub bouncer, card dealer at illegal gambling houses and all-around dandy. He was most prominent, however, as a well-regarded racetrack tout, which was the etymology of his nickname. Posing as a horse owner or other trafficker of inside information, Duffy would whisper a tip in the ear of an unsophisticated horse player.

"Bet fifty on him—and bet something for yourself," Duffy would say softly.

He would follow the mark to the betting window and collect his share of the tickets, his "fee," you might say, for sharing this valued advice. If he worked quickly and latched onto enough suckers, his pockets contained tickets on every horse in the race when the starting gates flew open. Duffy cashed after almost every race. Old-timers still speak of him fondly, this being the only business outside of Wall Street where such practices are acceptable, even admired.

Duffy was, in fact, a fine handicapper in his own right, which should not be dismissed. While driving home from the track once, he observed that a car appeared to be following him. He began to take a circuitous route up and down side streets and the car remained close behind. Finally, while stopped at a red light, a stranger leaped out of the car and rushed up to Duffy's side window.

Terrified, Duffy blurted out, "I don't have any money."

"I don't want your money," said the stranger. "All I want to know is who you like on tomorrow's card."

Naturally, Duffy had already studied the overnights and gave the stranger a tip or two at no charge. This was under duress, however, and should not count against him.

On the Christmas Eve in question, Duffy was genuinely moved by the holiday spirit. As the old-timers remember it, Duffy was studying *The Daily Racing Form* in a corner of the Backstage Club, a joint that flourished in the 1930s, when downtown Cleveland was considered a wicked city. Sharpies from the East would ride the New York Central and Pennsylvania Railroad to Cleveland for wild weekends of drinking and gambling. It may be hard to imagine, but it was true. Cleveland was the sixth-largest city in the country and it was quite exciting at that time.

While perusing the Christmas Day entries at the Fairgrounds in New Orleans, Duffy came across a horse named, "St. Nick."

Not even a crusty tout such as Duffy could ignore that kind of a hunch play and he could not resist sharing it with his friends.

And so, across the mirror behind the bar of the Backstage Club, Duffy scrawled in grease pencil, "St. Nick 5th race Fairgrounds Christmas Day."

Everybody in the joint jumped on it, especially the bar girls, who were employed at the Backstage Club to hustle over-priced, watered-down drinks. Duffy had a special affinity for the bar girls, since they were in the same profession.

It has been years since bookmakers took bets on horses, but in those days, the late 1930s, horse racing made up most of their business. The point spread had not been invented yet. It was still a decade away. If you wanted to bet Notre Dame over Drake in 1937 the odds were 1-20. You bet $20 to win a buck. There wasn't much action on games like that.

The clientele at the Backstage Club included many bookmakers, which made it convenient for the bar girls to make their wagers on St. Nick. They bet 50 cents to a dollar, which is a pittance today, but in the Depression that was a lot of money. The bar girls made only $17 a week and all they could steal from the patrons.

Needless to say, St. Nick won and he devastated the downtown bookies, who did not lay off their bets with the syndicate, the way they do now. What self-respecting bookie could take seriously the handicapping expertise of bar girls who got their tips from a backbar mirror? St. Nick went off at 30-1 and paid $60 at the Fairgrounds. Off the track, the bookies paid the limit: 20-1.

It was a very merry Christmas for the bar girls, who earned more than a week's wages for a $1 bet.

Duffy's heart was also warmed, a feeling that was quite foreign to him.

The moral of the story is clear. There is a Santa Claus and he operates under several names. In 1939 he used the non de plume Whispering John Duffy.

Chester Bright—Scratched

For no good reason, horse racing is called the sport of kings, which is ironic because the oldest axiom in the game is that all horse players die broke.

Chester Bright upheld that tradition to his dying day. When they found him frozen in the back seat of a car behind the Broadway Bar, he had 39 cents in his pocket.

Bright, who was 67, worked as a groom for many years at Thistledown Racetrack. He walked hots, rubbed down the horses, fed them and shoveled their manure. After having a few drinks at night, he would snuggle up on a mound of hay and sleep with the horses. There are sleeping quarters for grooms in the barn area, but when they were filled Chester was just as comfortable with the horses.

He was quite content with his life. He had an agreeable nature and got along well with everyone. He liked people as much as he liked horses. He was usually unshaven and his clothes were rarely washed, but he had a friendly smile.

In the afternoons, when he slipped out of the barn area to make his bets at the mutuel windows, he would wave to his pals and pat the wallet in his hip pocket. "I'm gonna get the money, honey," he would say.

He usually did. He was one of the finest sources of inside information at the racetrack.

"Oh, yes," said Junior O'Malley, the gambler and raconteur, "he was pretty sharp with the horses. He was quite a character. When he had money, he'd give you the shirt off his back. When he was broke, he'd bum you for the price of a drink or a sandwich."

Chester's only mailing address was the barn. When Thistledown closed in the winter and the horses shipped out, so did Chester. During the harsh Cleveland winters he slept wherever he could.

"Don't worry. I got plenty of cardboard," he said.

Sometimes he told people he slept in a different motel each night.

"The Eldorado Motel, the Ford Motel, the Chevy Motel, which-ever car happened to be unlocked," he said with a smile.

"To you and me, this sounds like a sorrowful existence," said Junior, "but he was happy. Sure he was. He was a happy-go-lucky guy. There are a lot of grooms like that.

"I wouldn't want to do it," Junior continued. "When I was 15 years old I ran away from home for the 14th time. I rode in a railroad car with racehorses from the old Bainbridge Racetrack to New Orleans. I wouldn't want to do it today, but there are a lot of people who think it's very normal to sleep with horses all their lives.

"All he wanted was his action. He had his thrills. Every time one of his horses ran, he got his thrills. There are a lot of people who go home to warm houses every night and sleep on clean sheets and never have any thrills. These are the people I feel sorry for.

"I'm sorry about one thing," Junior said suddenly. "I always thought he'd die with his boots on at the track. That's the way a lot of grooms go. They find them dead one morning on a bale of hay. That's how Chester should have checked out. It would have been proper. But he probably never gave it much thought.

"He had a lot of winners and he had some losers. He was prob-ably happier than a lot of people who never took a chance in their lives. If he had his life to live over, I think he'd do it the same way. Believe me, I do."

His epitaph was simple. Chester Bright, scratched.

Twenty-one mutuel clerks at Thistledown took up a collection and raised $135 so that Chester would be buried in a warm blanket. They sent the money out with Junior and me. It was a lousy morning, not that cold, but misty and wet and we figured we'd get mud all over ourselves so we didn't go to the cemetery. We went directly to the saloon. I threw the money on the bar and told everybody to have a drink on Chester.

"Chester never had it so good," said Junior.

Everybody had just returned from Calvary Cemetery, where Father Clarence Korgie from St. Stanislaus Church said a few prayers and blessed the casket. About 20 of Chester's friends from the racetrack stood around in the mud and the mist and said their "Amens."

"It was a very classy operation. Chester would have been proud of himself," observed John Zupanc.

"He also would have been surprised," added Art Spath.

Dan Cegelka had the idea that everybody should have another drink on Chester, so they did.

"Chester owes me," said Cegelka, who recalled that every day Chester would make his rounds in the South East Chevrolet service department collecting $2 bets on the afternoon's races.

"For a week straight I bet the daily double. He'd take my two bucks and walk across the street to the Broadway Café and spend it on top-shelf whisky. He never put my bets in. He didn't think I'd win. After a week I hit the double. Forty dollars. He said he'd owe me."

Cegelka never carried a grudge. Just the opposite, he started a fund to bury the old groom.

"He had nothing and he was headed for an unmarked grave in potter's field," said Cegelka. "He deserved better than that."

Several people got involved. Tony LaRiche, who owned South East Chevrolet, made a deal with Eddie Kotecki, the monument man. LaRiche traded a used Corvair to Kotecki in exchange for a nice grave marker. The cost of the plot and the grave diggers was extra, so Beverly Lindeman, who worked as a bartender at the Broadway Café, collected $200 from her customers. The money poured in. There was no stopping it. The Horsemen's Benevolent and Protective Association said they would make up any deficit. Another man who insisted on anonymity said he would pick up the tab for the whole thing but most of the costs had been covered already.

Cegelka went for a better grade of casket and still had money left over. No more cardboard for Chester. Cegelka ordered a party tray for the gang at the Broadway Café and he gave the rest of the money to Chester's sister, Dorothy Forsythe, whose husband had died two weeks earlier.

"Chester always said he had a bunch of friends," said Cegelka.

What was this man's attraction? He was a mooch. He rarely bathed and people literally could smell him coming.

Eddie Lynch, a young trainer at Thistlcdown at the time, leaned against the bar and spread his sport coat, revealing a big, silver belt buckle with the raised image of a horse.

"He gave it to me," said Lynch. "He had nothing, but somehow he got the money to buy this belt buckle for me."

Lynch's eyes were very misty at that moment.

He was a happy person and he made other people happy," said Lynch. "What he had, he shared."

The windshield wipers were clearing a path through the drizzle as we drove back downtown. Junior O'Malley looked straight ahead. Finally he broke the silence.

"The bottom line on your ledger is whether you were a nice guy," said Junior. "It doesn't matter how successful a person is, how famous he is or how much money he makes. If he isn't remembered as being a nice guy, he's nothing."

The Sport of Kings

The one thing all horse players have in common is hope. Even after they have lost everything else, they still have hope. If they could package it, they could feed the world.

Take the vaudeville comedian Joe Frisco. When he ran into Bing Crosby at a Hollywood breakfast diner, Frisco had only bus fare in his pocket.

"Can you loan me a sawbuck until tonight?" Frisco asked.

"If you don't plan on losing it at Santa Anita," Crosby said as he handed Frisco a $10 bill.

Frisco had no intention of losing it. No horse player ever goes to the track with a defeatist attitude. He rode the bus to Santa Anita and then jumped on one winner after another. Frisco enjoyed the hottest streak of his life. After nine races he had parlayed $10 into almost $1,000. On that one day, he was invincible. The particular horse he had been following was in the tenth race and Joe put every last dollar on its nose. The horse, alas, stumbled coming out of the gate. The jockey fell off and the horse finished last.

As Frisco walked out of the track and headed for the bus stop, an acquaintance came up to him.

"How'd you do, Joe?" he asked.

"Oh, I lost 10 bucks," said Frisco.

*   *   *

One of the best handicappers I ever knew was a Catholic priest, Monsignor Edward F. Seward. In January 1972, he leaned close to my ear and whispered, "Riva Ridge." That was all. He said, "Riva Ridge." This was based on the horse's brief two-year-old campaign. He had not yet run as a three-year-old. Well, Riva Ridge won the Kentucky Derby and the Preakness and finished a close second in the Belmont Stakes.

Monsignor Seward was pastor of St. Clement Church, where he was known for his insightful homilies. Needless to say, I was all ears when I ran into the monsignor the following year at our favorite meeting spot, the Blue Fox restaurant. That was well before the feds shut it down for giving aid and comfort to bookmakers.

"Secretariat," Monsignor Seward said.

It didn't take a Jeremiah to spot Secretariat. The big horse became the first steed in 25 years to win the Triple Crown. He didn't merely win it. He dominated the Kentucky Derby, Preakness and Belmont Stakes. He won the Belmont Stakes by 31½ lengths over a mile and a half, two furlongs longer than the Kentucky Derby. On any reputable list of great thoroughbreds, Secretariat is second only to Man o' War. As with Riva Ridge, however, Monsignor Seward anointed Secretariat for greatness after only a handful of races as a two-year-old, before most people had heard of him.

When Secretariat died, they did an autopsy and discovered that his heart was twice the size of normal horses'. When Monsignor Seward died, no autopsy was necessary. We took it on blind faith that he knew what he was talking about.

*   *   *

I have a framed picture of Secretariat and me taken in the pasture of his retirement farm. I'm standing next to the great horse with my right arm around his neck. I don't know why he allowed me to do that because he didn't like people very much.

An old black groom who took me out to see the magnificent creature told me to be careful.

"He'll try to bite you. Watch out for your hands. He'll bite your finger off. He's a mean one," said the old groom.

I glanced down and noticed that the groom was missing two fingers from his right hand.

*   *   *

In the mid-1960s when the Indians games were televised by WJW-TV, the Kentucky Derby was on the same station. Inevitably, a ball game went into extra innings on the first Saturday in May. We had a television set with rabbit ears in *The Plain Dealer* sports department and we watched pensively to see how WJW-TV would handle its predicament. As post time for the Derby grew closer, the Indians were still playing in the 12th inning.

The phones began to ring. Racing fans demanded to know if they were going to see their Derby. When people had a complaint about their television programs, they usually called the newspaper. We never knew why. Would they call *The Press* if they didn't get their *Plain Dealer*? Would they call a Ford dealer if their Chevrolet broke down?

I was answering the phones fast and furious, telling callers to bother Channel 8, but one woman refused to back down. She wanted to know if Channel 8 would switch to the horse race and she wanted to know now.

As the horses were entering the starting gates, Channel 8 cut away from the baseball game and switched to the Kentucky Derby.

"Madam, can you see your television set?" I asked her.

"No, it's in the other room," she said.

"Good," I said.

The race started and I allowed her to complain for two minutes and three seconds.

"Madam," I said. "You just missed it."

My Move to the Press— A Stroke of Genius

In its final days, the *Cleveland Press* did some illogical things. On one hand, the reporters and editors took pay cuts to keep the paper alive. On the other hand, money was foolishly wasted. We're still scratching our heads.

For example, the *Press* offered buyouts to reduce its payroll. Then the new owner decided to start a Sunday morning edition to compete with *The Plain Dealer* for those huge Sunday advertising dollars. New workers were hired to put out the Sunday edition, which debuted in April, 1981. Advertising director Bob Hatton believed the paper was headed in the right direction.

There were other implausible developments. In the spring of 1981 *Press* editor Herb Kamm called me at home. Having failed to lure Hal Lebovitz away from *The Plain Dealer*, the *Press* now targeted me. I knew Herb. He was a nice enough guy. Maddy and I agreed to listen to his proposal over dinner at the Kamms' apartment in Bratenahl Place. It's hard to forget the night. It was Good Friday, the most solemn day on the Christian calendar, but you still go to work and do business. You even have clandestine meetings sometimes.

"Can't have meat," I reminded him. "Catholics can't eat meat on Fridays during Lent, especially on Good Friday."

As though an urbane Jewish guy from New York didn't already know that. We were probably going to have a kosher fish dinner anyway.

All week I walked around *The Plain Dealer* with a guilty conscience, unable to look anybody in the eye. People in the news business hate secrets and I had a big one. By Thursday I couldn't hold it in any longer. I went into the office of Dave Hopcraft, editor of *The Plain Dealer*, who I mistakenly believed was a friend of mine.

"Herb Kamm is going to make me an offer tomorrow night," I said to Hopcraft. "Could we work out something right now so I won't even have to listen to the offer? I can cancel the meeting."

How stupid I was. I thought there were only two ways he could react.

First, "We don't want to lose you. Stay put. Don't go anywhere. We'll do something to keep you."

Second, "I won't get into a bidding war. Do what you have to do. Good luck."

He didn't say any of those things. Instead, he went in a third direction.

"If he steals you, I'll steal every good man he has," Hopcraft blustered.

Had he forgotten that he started this war? He had already stolen political writer Brent Larkin and investigative reporter Walt Bogdanich from *The Press* and he tried to purloin Dick Feagler.

Years later, Hopcraft said he didn't remember saying that, which is possible. Who can remember every conversation from long ago? Actually, I do. I remember it because to me it was a major event in my life. Herb Kamm also remembered it.

That night Kamm called me at home. He didn't even say hello.

"What the hell is going on?" he thundered.

I stammered it all out, about going in to see Hopcraft.

"He called me and raised hell," said Kamm. "He said if I stole you, he'd steal every good man I had."

Was there an echo?

"Forget about tomorrow night. It's off," said Kamm.

I was embarrassed because I had violated the confidence of a secret meeting. Afterward I never talked to anyone about the episode except my father-in-law, who said Hopcraft was right. Keep in mind that my father-in-law was a CEO. He ran a medium-sized corporation. Everyone loved him. He took care of his family very well. That's all I wanted to do—take care of my family very well. Maddy and I were expecting our first baby and there was a very good chance more would be on the way.

Almost a full year went by and in March 1982, while I was touring the baseball spring training camps in Florida, *Press* sports editor Peter Bloomfield woke me up with an early morning phone call. I never found out how he located me. I was in a different hotel every night as I went from training camp to training camp. That morning I was in the Cincinnati Reds' hotel in Tampa. Bloomfield's voice had an urgent tone.

"We have to talk as soon as you get back," he said.

I called Maddy and told her but that was all. I said nothing to anybody else. When I got home I even avoided the Headliner Bar so that my tongue would not be loosened by barley and hops. That was a first.

This time the meeting was at my house and Bloomfield was the point man. He came for lunch. Maddy made short ribs and we ate in the kitchen. Bloomfield laid out their plan to make me the sports columnist. Bob August, an exquisite writer, had given up the sports column and was writing senior citizen pieces. Bob Sudyk replaced August but he left for New Haven, Conn. When Doug Clarke assumed the sports columnist position I thought they were in pretty good shape, but Bloomfield said they wanted two of us. Bloomfield had all the answers except one—how much were they offering? He kept lobbing the ball back into my court.

"What will it take?" he asked.

How much did they have? I wondered.

"Listen, Peter," I said, "the most important thing is lifetime security. I like the job I have now and I'll have it for life. How can the *Press* guarantee that?"

"I'll get back to you on that," he said.

In the meantime I called an old friend, Cleveland sports agent Ed Keating, who was at the peak of his prowess. His list of clients included Dick Butkus, Larry Csonka, Jim Kiick, Brian Sipe, Frank Robinson, Buddy Bell, Rick Manning, Duane Kuiper, Wayne Garland, Dennis Eckersley and George Hendrick, to name just a few.

According to magazine writer Diana Tittle, who covered the story for *Northern Ohio Live,* I said to Keating, "When you're 43 and you're still worried about making mortgage payments on a little three bedroom in Lakewood—shouldn't I be doing better than this?" Keating said, "Yes."

I'm grateful to Diana because her story jogged my memory.

Keating counseled me about getting those annoying little details in writing but he insisted, "My role wasn't that of a hired gunslinger."

Nevertheless, the *Press* was afraid of him.

"We didn't want to get into formal negotiations with a lawyer," the *Press'* new executive editor Bill DiMascio told her.

After several days Bloomfield called again. The urgency was back in his voice. He needed a number. This was a neat trick and I fell for

it. Instead of the *Press* making an offer, they tricked me into starting the bidding, reversing the roles of the pursuer and the pursuee.

So I took a base salary, multiplied it by 25 years and said that's
what the *Press* owed me, about $1.25 million dollars. I would work
it off one year at a time. On the surface, it seemed outrageous, but
it wasn't. It was what I would earn over the course of my working
career. I didn't even allow for inflation. Actually, they were getting
the family discount. I simply wanted the *Press* to guarantee it. If
the *Press* went out of business in the next quarter of a century they
would owe me for what was left. If I died, however, they were off
the hook. It probably wasn't a smart arrangement on my part. They
couldn't fire me but they could bump me off. I can imagine how the
order would come down. "Kill the column on C-1." Anyway, when
Bloomfield took it to his bosses, they almost had heart attacks.

A few days later we had an early morning meeting in the closed,
darkened restaurant of the Holiday Inn next door to the *Press*. To
continue the metaphor, they were deadly serious. The *Press* was represented by Kamm, associate publisher Jerry Merlino and DiMascio,
who was brought in from the Associated Press as executive editor
the previous summer. Kamm had become editor emeritus.

This time they had a proposal. A significant salary, much more
than I was making at *The Plain Dealer,* and a signing bonus of half
a year's pay in cash. It was time for serious thinking. Maddy and I
were expecting our second baby and we needed a bigger house.

After several more days, Kamm called on the phone and said,
"You're crazy if you don't take it."

Merlino, who had recently joined owner Joe Cole as associate
publisher, had grand plans to increase advertising. He was likable
and he was convincing. Hal Lebovitz always said, "Life is full of
adventures." So, what the hell? I said yes.

We set up a meeting for Saturday morning, April 3, in the downtown offices of lawyer Robert Duvin, whose firm represented the
paper. I had the proverbial funny feeling in the pit of my stomach.
This was life-changing. *The Plain Dealer* was my comfort zone. My
good friends were there. But we needed a bigger house and the thrill
of a new adventure kicked in. They presented a contract typed up
with everything we had agreed on.

On my side was my brother-in-law, Craig Andrews, a corporation lawyer in real life. He scanned the contract. It looked fine. But

I questioned one thing. It was a three-year contract. The subject of a time limit had never come up in our conversations, especially one as short as three years. This was no time for surprises. I didn't like that and I balked. I wanted an open-ended contract, one that was in force as long as the paper and I were alive. I thought that was clear.

"To be a valid contract, you need a starting date and an ending date," said Craig Brown, a young lawyer from Duvin's firm.

Craig Andrews didn't seem concerned about that.

"Let it go. Sign the deal," said Craig.

So I did and the three-year limit turned out to be a blessing. The *Press* wound up paying me for three full years without bickering over every little detail. The check came the first of every month and I already had the signing bonus in the bank.

The following Monday when I handed my resignation letter to Hopcraft, he blurted out, "They're going out of business." Hal Lebovitz said the same thing. Everybody in the world knew that, but who knew it would happen so soon?

According to Tittle's story in *Northern Ohio Live,* Hopcraft was bitter and loud. She quoted one staff member as saying, "He was angry that Dan would be so mercenary and abandon ship."

It was his turn to be blindsided.

All this blindsiding went back and forth. Less than three months later—two months and two weeks, actually—*The Plain Dealer* bought the *Press,* shut it down and ripped out the computer wiring in the newsroom so nobody could start a new paper in the building.

In retrospect, I admit I got fooled. I actually believed the *Press* was going to last for a few years—not forever, certainly, but a few years—because Jerry Merlino and Bill DiMascio seemed to believe. Now I believe Joe Cole had other ideas. It's too late now. The central figures are dead.

In 1984, two years after the sellout, Marilyn A. Bobula, a lawyer in the Antitrust Division of the U.S. Justice Department, called me to talk about the demise of the *Press.* The Justice Department had launched an investigation and Bobula was one of two lead lawyers. She wanted to know what I knew. She wanted to know how I fit into the puzzle. I don't know, I told her, and that was the truth. She wanted to meet with me. I said it would be a waste of her time. I saw nothing that made me suspicious. As Joe Cole said in his "goodbye" editorial, a recession had hit Cleveland and "the times simply were against us." Besides, my checks were coming on schedule the first of every month and I was not going to screw it up by standing on the courthouse steps demanding an investigation. She phoned several times. In 1987 the Justice Department dropped the investigation for "lack of evidence." I never met lawyer Bobula, which I regret because now I believe she was on to something.

"You were their defense. You were their cover," my lawyer Craig Andrews says now. "When they guaranteed you the money, it supported their intention to remain in business."

The Justice Department probe was triggered by two former *Press* investigative reporters, Dan Cook and Peter Phipps, who in January 1984 churned out a series in the *Akron Beacon-Journal* that illuminated a curious relationship between *Press* owner Joe Cole and *Plain Dealer* owner S.I. Newhouse.

Among their revelations, which never were denied, was that in December 1980, only months after Joe Cole bought the *Press*, he called Newhouse at his Florida home and requested a meeting. Cole apparently realized that buying the paper was a mistake after his auditors went through the books and concluded that the *Press* was doomed. Cole had heard of joint publishing agreements, although he didn't know exactly how they worked, and he hoped such an arrangement with *The Plain Dealer* would save the *Press*. Newhouse, however, had no interest in saving the *Press*.

I joined the *Press* on April 5, 1982, and by June it was in crisis mode, especially after they got my expense account from the Cooney-Holmes heavyweight championship fight in Las Vegas. They might have lasted another week if I had stayed home. On the other hand, they were almost out of newsprint and the paper mills in Canada had cut off their credit. In another week they might have run out of paper in the middle of the run.

							*	*	*

Ralph Arraj, the bartender at the Communicators' Club in the Statler Office Tower, said men were crying when they walked out of a meeting there the night of June 16, 1982. The top executives of the *Cleveland Press* had just learned the newspaper was finished and that its bitter rival, *The Plain Dealer*, would carve up the cadaver. It was like the signing of Japan's unconditional surrender on the deck of the battleship Missouri in Tokyo Harbor in 1945. Men and women who had spent decades at the *Press*, their entire lives, could not hold back the tears. That's one thing the *Press* had. It had spirit; it had camaraderie. It really was a family. Even as an outsider, I could recognize that.

The rumor had leaked out earlier that evening on Channel 8's six o'clock news, where Herb Kamm had only recently become "editorial director." By 11 p.m. all the stations had it. At 7 a.m. the next morning somebody posted a statement on the bulletin board in the middle of the city room saying the edition of Thursday, June 17, 1982, would be the last. My phone at home rang at 7:01 a.m. It was Jerry Merlino saying I had nothing to worry about. The *Press* would fulfill its obligations to me. Additionally, I was free to pursue any other opportunities. Don't feel sorry for me.

Don't feel sorry for Joe Cole. He bought the *Press* for $1 million in 1980 and he sold it to S.I. Newhouse two years later for $14.5 million plus another $8 million for Del-Com, the advertising supplement. That's $22.5 million. And Cole kept the building, which later was torn down to make room for a new office building on prime land at the corner of East Ninth Street and Lakeside Avenue. My monthly check, by the way, came out of that $22.5 million.

In the end, the *Cleveland Press* printed nothing but money for Joe Cole.

During the final negotiations Merlino asked that *The Plain Dealer* rehire me. The answer wasn't no. It was an emphatic no. Furthermore, Dave Hopcraft said he would not hire anyone from the editorial side of the *Press*, although over the next few years several former reporters and editors trickled over.

* * *

The timing of the sale was critical for *The Plain Dealer* because its contract with the Teamsters Union expired in August and negotiations were not going well. The Teamsters knew that a strike at *The Plain Dealer* would breathe life into the *Press* and they used that for leverage. At the same time, Joe Cole used the Teamsters as leverage to sweeten his deal. Negotiations between the Teamsters and *The Plain Dealer* dragged on even after the demise of the *Press*, which generated hope that a new afternoon paper could emerge from the ruins of a strike. The Teamsters were the key to Cleveland's newspaper future.

Waiting in the wings was Dave Skylar, who had been Howard Metzenbaum's partner when they owned the chain of *Sun Newspapers*. We met early one morning at a downtown coffee shop. He wanted me to put together an editorial staff ready to go to work on a moment's notice.

"If there's a strike, I want a paper up and running almost immediately," Skylar said. "It's the only way a startup newspaper would have a chance to survive. You can't go head to head with *The Plain Dealer* unless you have a head start."

The Teamsters eventually settled. The strike was averted and any hope of launching a new afternoon paper was dead. Cleveland was officially a one-newspaper town.

"By the way," Skylar said during our last meeting, "I'm the one who really put the *Press* out of business. I'm not bragging about it. I'm not happy about it. But it's a fact. When Howard and I bought up the suburban weeklies and created the *Sun* chain, we stole the classified advertising from the *Press*. We didn't affect the *Plain Dealer*, but we stole the guts out of the *Press*. That's what killed it. That wasn't our plan. That's just the way it happened."

Ironically, if the Teamsters had called a strike for the purpose of nurturing a new afternoon paper, they would have created more union jobs but anti-trust lawyer Bobula would have come around with a fistful of subpoenas. I don't think anybody suggested such a thing. Maybe they thought it, but they didn't say it. Just the threat, however, was a weapon and the Teamsters used it wisely.

*   *   *

Joe Cole sold the *Press* 20 months after he bought it. When it closed, it had 900 employees and a daily circulation of 316,147, which ranked in the top 25 of American newspapers. Its final edition had 56 pages and a four-page advertising insert, roughly twice the size of the typical *Plain Dealer* weekday edition in the year 2010.

I Replaced Gary Dee—and WHK Never Recovered

Within 48 hours of the demise of *The Press* I had a job offer. Gil Rosenwald called me at home. Gil was president of Malrite Broadcasting, owner of WHK-AM and WMMS-FM, and he knew exactly what he wanted. I trotted down to his office in the Statler Office Tower at East 12th St. and Euclid Avenue. He introduced me to Ron Jones, general manager of WHK, who outlined their plan.

"We have in mind a daily sports commentary—two or three minutes. It will run at 7:55 in the morning on the Gary Dee show on WHK. You'll do it live from your home. We'll put a radio line into your house. We'll record it and rerun it at five o'clock on the Joe Finan show. We'll pay you $20,000 a year," said Jones.

Just like that, he covered everything. This was so weird. When I was in college I worked on the student radio station and I wasn't very good. I called play-by-play on Notre Dame baseball and basketball games. My partner, Tim Ryan, was destined for stardom. He later worked NFL games for CBS. Tim was all-pro. I was semi-pro. I had no future in broadcasting. I hungered to be a newspaperman.

But when Ron Jones started throwing numbers around, such as 20 grand, it changed my thinking. Within a few days AT&T engineers were in my basement turning my Lakewood house into a radio studio. They ran cables through the walls to an upstairs bedroom. When they were finished wiring me up I could have dialed up Radio Free Europe. Give me the area code and I could have talked to the Space Shuttle.

The only bad thing was the 7:55 a.m. part. I wasn't a morning person. I was a night person. Those were my genes, but things were changing. We had one baby with another on the way. If the deal was 7:55 a.m., that was it. I had responsibility now. So before going to bed at night, I would type out my commentary. When the alarm went off at 7:54 I would bounce up, walk into the next room, listen for my cue, throw the switch on the microphone and go on the air in my underwear. I was able to do this without waking up entirely, thereby allowing me to go right back to sleep. I liked radio.

This went on for about 14 months. In the middle of September, Maddy and I spent my birthday in South Bend, Ind., at the Notre Dame-Michigan State game. Aunt Josie watched the boys. We had two of them by now. When we got back Sunday night, Josie said that Ron Jones had called. He wanted me to call him first thing Monday morning.

"They're probably going to fire me," I said. "That's all right. We're doing well."

I was grateful. They had paid me about 25 grand and I didn't even have to get dressed. That's a nice racket.

After doing my Monday morning commentary, I stayed awake until Jones got in the office. I called him.

"You've gotta come down here for a meeting at ten o'clock," he said.

"Listen, Ron, if you're going to fire me, that's all right. Don't make me drive down there and pay five bucks to park in the lot next to the Union Club," I said.

Some people are insulted if they're fired over the phone. That's what really irritated Bob Neal when Nick Mileti let him go as the Indians' play-by-play announcer in 1972. Neal was furious.

"He didn't do it in person. He called me up and did it on the phone," Neal complained to me.

I never thought about the protocol of getting fired. I never thought there was a right way or a wrong way. You're fired. That's it. I imagine people are now getting fired by text message. People in radio get fired all the time. It's expected.

Jones was insistent. I had to attend the meeting.

"OK, I'll be there by ten o'clock," I said.

What the hell. I rationalized it. They had paid me about 25 grand and I didn't even have to get dressed and go to work. It would have been unseemly to make an issue over five bucks to park, even if he was going to fire me.

We waited for program director Bill Stedman to finish his shift at ten o'clock. Stedman was filling in for morning man Gary Dee, who was on vacation. Stedman, Jones and I then went downstairs to Swingos Restaurant on the first floor of the Statler Office Tower. We sat at a table with linen napkins and a linen tablecloth and ordered coffee. It was a little early to start drinking, even for radio people.

Something was fishy. I got the feeling that they weren't going to fire me. What was up?

"We're going to fire Gary Dee and you're going to replace him," Ron Jones said.

I was shocked. Gary Dee was the biggest single performer in Cleveland radio.

"Oh, no," I countered. "I like the deal I have."

"You may not always have that deal," said Jones.

He could be a persuasive devil. Stedman finished the week. When Dee's vacation was over, they told him not to come back to work. They gave me a new contract and I went on the air at six o'clock the next Monday morning as part of a two-man team with Stedman playing country music. I had never listened to country music although in 1954 I liked Eddie Arnold's hit song, "Cattle Call." I wondered what I was doing. Within one year, I went from covering Notre Dame football to playing country music.

"Why?" I pestered Stedman. As the program director, he was involved in the palace coup. Gary Dee's ratings were still strong. The only station close to him was WMMS, the other Malrite station which was on the other side of the hallway. They were tucked together side-by-side. They even shared the same unisex restroom. There was a lot of testosterone strutting up and down that corridor. They were good and they knew it. Those two stations owned the market—1 and 1A.

"Here's what's going on," Stedman said. "Gary Dee is hurting sales. Some advertisers don't want to be associated with him. They're starting to boycott both WHK and WMMS."

"Besides," Stedman added, "Gary's ratings are starting to erode."

Gary was Cleveland's first shock jock. For the 1970s and 1980s he was racially outrageous and highly controversial. Some people found him offensive, but many others thought he was hilarious. And suddenly he wasn't there. I was.

Stedman was my partner for only a couple of weeks, until Johnny Douglas signed on. He was a top 40 jock who went a mile a minute. That lasted a month and then they brought in Bill Garcia from Charlotte, N.C., to work with me.

Since I was the only constant in this experiment, I take credit for destroying the oldest radio station in Cleveland. I took WHK's morning drive ratings—the lifeblood of a radio station—from 7.5 to 1.5 in six months. It had to be a record. Not only did I take them from the penthouse to the outhouse in record time, but they even changed their format. In March, six months after I became a morning man, WHK changed its name to 14-K and changed its entire format from country music to old time rock 'n' roll and my disc jockey days were mercifully over.

The Ugliest Guy on Television

When Beano Cook retired from ABC, I strolled through the Channel 8 newsroom announcing, "Here I am, everybody. The ugliest man left on television."

Lou Maglio stood up at his desk and argued.

"No, you're not," Lou declared. "I knew a guy in Cedar Rapids who was uglier than you."

We doubled over in laughter. It became a regular routine. The joke was, what was a guy who looked like me doing in a business like this, a business where you powdered your nose before going on the air?

And those were the guys!

The last place I ever thought I'd work is a television station. I told you about my failed radio career in college. I tried it and I wasn't very good. Basically, I was a newspaper animal. I couldn't pass a newsstand without stopping to read the headlines, study the layout and scan a story or two.

I wasn't even a good television viewer. I spent my nights either covering games, writing stories in the newspaper office or holding forth in bars. I knew that WKYC (Channel 3) was the NBC affiliate because Johnny Carson was on Channel 3. As for the other two, I never knew how ABC and CBS matched up with WEWS (Channel 5) and WJW (Channel 8).

Win Smith, the assignment editor at WKYC, called in 1972.

"We want to talk to you about a job," he said.

Win suggested meeting for lunch with WKYC news director Roy Wetzel at Marie Schreiber's restaurant in the Hollenden House Hotel at East Sixth Street and Superior Avenue.

They needed a weekend sports anchor, which meant quitting *The Plain Dealer* and I wasn't keen on that.

"You'll make more money. You'll double your salary," Wetzel said.

That was believable. They did not mention a number but it wouldn't take much to double my pay at *The Plain Dealer*.

"But I like my newspaper job," I said.

"Do people ask for your autograph?" Win asked.

"Of course not," I said.

"When you're on television, people come up to you and ask for your autograph when you walk down the street," Win said.

I stared at them incredulously.

"Did you ever see me on WVIZ?" I asked.

For a couple of years I had done three-minute commentaries on Mike Massa's high school sports program on WVIZ, Cleveland's public television station. I stood at a podium and read from a script. It fell barely short of network quality.

"I didn't know that," said Wetzel.

"See, he's got experience," said Win.

"Why me?" I asked.

"We like the way you write," Win said.

"If you can hire somebody as easy as this, you can fire him just as easy," I said.

I politely declined. It was a smart decision. I would have flopped terribly.

A few days later Wetzel also made a smart decision. He hired Joe Castiglione from Youngstown and Joe worked in the Cleveland market for 11 years until becoming the radio voice of the Boston Red Sox. He's still there, more than 25 years later, in the Fenway Park radio booth.

"Roy said he liked me because I didn't shout," Castiglione wrote in his book a few years ago.

But Channel 3 got even with me in the end. They turned me down twice.

On June 17, 1982, the day the *Press* folded, I was sitting in Pat Joyce's Tavern downtown with Channel 3's two news anchors, Doug Adair and Mona Scott, who were commiserating with my plight.

"How long were you there?" Mona asked.

"Two months and two weeks," I said.

"Maybe *The Plain Dealer* will hire you," Mona said hopefully.

"I don't think so," I said. "They're mad at me."

"Why is that?" Mona asked.

"I used to work there and I quit," I said.

"Why did you quit?" she pressed on.

"To work for *The Press*," I said.

"Oh, I see," she said.

Ed Keating, the sports agent, came in and joined us. Doug and Mona thought it would be a good idea if I went to work for Channel 3. Keating agreed and said he would try to put the deal together.

Doug and Mona pitched the thought that afternoon to their news director, Kris Ostrowski, who had no interest. Keating called station manager Neal Van Ells who said the well was dry. Revenue was down and his budget was maxed out.

WEWS Channel 5, however, held auditions in their studio for any *Press* employee who wanted to try out. About a dozen of us did. I was very impressed with feature writer Norm Mlachak's approach. He pounded his right fist into a baseball glove on his left hand and told a poignant story about growing up with baseball. "Damn, that's good," I thought. "I wish I had thought of using a prop."

Me, I just stood there and did a commentary the way I did on WVIZ a decade earlier. The only person Channel 5 hired from *The Press* was gossip columnist Harriet Peters for the noon news and "Live on Five." She lasted only a few months.

"It didn't translate well onto television," Harriet said.

She should have used props.

WJW Channel 8 had shown absolutely no interest in hiring *Press* people but that's where my seeds of opportunity were sown. Keating contacted news director Virgil Dominic.

"My problem is that I have no openings in news and no budget for additional hires at this time," he wrote back to Keating. "I have spoken to Mary Horth of our 'PM Magazine' unit and she indicated a strong interest in Dan. I have given her your number and she's promised to call."

Channel 8's "PM Magazine" show was a ratings blockbuster that did a highly flattering six-minute story on me shortly after I made the move from *The Plain Dealer* to the *Press*. Co-host Jim Finnerty told the story, photographer Bob Kasarda shot it and John Cifani was the sound engineer. It aired two weeks before the *Press* closed.

When the rubble cleared, Cifani approached Mary Horth, who was executive producer of "PM Magazine," and suggested they use me on the show. Mary was the boss but she got along like a co-worker. Everybody who worked on that show had great camaraderie.

"He did pretty well when we interviewed him," Cifani pointed out.

Virgil Dominic's endorsement heightened her interest.

"We could try him," Mary agreed and soon I was on the air.

I knew nothing. Two Channel 8 producers, Nina Hickey and Jim Felber, alternated working with me. Nina was first. She would "scout" the story, do the interviews, write the scripts and then coach me in speaking my lines.

"Memorize these three sentences," she would say. "Now, walk from here to there, look at the camera and say those three lines. Don't shout. The microphone is right here on your tie."

We would do that three or four times, then move on to the next three or four sentences.

"Say two sentences and then reach down and pick up the apple and say the next two lines while you're looking at the apple. Keep looking at the apple," she would say.

"This is the damnedest business," I often said. "I'm supposed to be the writer, but now I'm just another pretty face. A young lady writes my scripts. I powder my nose and recite her words and I get nominated for an Emmy. Don't tell anybody how it works or everybody will want to do it."

My first year I actually did get nominated for an Emmy. I didn't win, but if I had won I was going to call Nina up to the stage and hand her the statuette and blow the cover off the entire business.

I did win an Emmy the second year, but I kept it because I actually did contribute to the story about the 20th anniversary of the 1964 Browns. The Emmy is a doorstop in my home office, an idea borrowed from Terry Baker, the 1962 Heisman Trophy winner.

"Where do you keep the Heisman Trophy?" I asked Baker years ago when I was talking to him on the phone.

"I'm looking at it," he said. "I use it as the doorstop in my office."

Channel 8 offered me a full-time contract to cover sports in 1985, the same week I received my last check from the Cleveland Press Liquidation Fund. What a coincidence. It was a month after my deal to return to *The Plain Dealer* collapsed.

On the last Friday in June, 1985, *The Plain Dealer's* executive editor Bill Woestendiek called me at home. It was quite a surprise. He was fairly new. We had never met.

"People have said we should talk," he said. "Would you be interested in returning to *The Plain Dealer*?"

"Very much," I said eagerly.

We met the following Monday and talked about money.

"Bill, I've got three little kids and a big mortgage. I need fifty grand," I said. That was $15,000 above union scale. He said that was no problem.

He called sports editor Thom Greer on the phone and asked him to walk down to his office. He told Greer that I would be coming on board.

"Welcome," said Thom. We shook hands. We knew each other from his earlier stint at the paper in the mid-1970s. Everything seemed fine.

Things got weird quickly, however. Back in the sports department, Greer told the copy editors that he didn't want any of my "funny stuff" getting in the paper. Hmmm. He wasn't entirely on board.

I ran into Hal Lebovitz, who was gone from *The Plain Dealer* but still had sources within the paper. He said there was no way they were taking me back.

"But, Hal, we shook on a deal," I protested.

"It won't happen," he said.

And it didn't. Woestendiek had been in Cleveland for only 15 months and didn't know the history. It never occurred to him that he would have to hold a board of directors meeting to bring me back. Roy Kopp, the paper's business manager, was against me and he was a powerful force, but he wasn't the only one.

I called Woestendiek and he sounded uncomfortable. The money, he said, was a problem.

"The $50,000 isn't there?" I said.

"No," he said.

We shadowboxed around the salary issue.

"What about $45,000?" I said.

"No, I don't think so," he said.

"Forty?" I kept going down.

"No," he said.

It was obvious what was going on. Top management had backed Woestendiek against a wall and ordered him not to hire me. I felt sorry for Woestendiek. He had called me with sincere intentions and now he had to renege on our agreement. He was embarrassed. The strategy was to reduce the salary until I turned down the job.

"What are you saying, union scale?" I said.

"Yes," he said softly.

"Well, let me talk to my wife about this. I'll call you back tomorrow," I said.

"I thought you said you needed $50,000. You said you couldn't live on less," he said. He sounded terrified, afraid that I might still take the job.

On one hand, I hungered to get back in the daily newspaper business, but on the other hand the welcome mat was rolled up and tucked away out of sight. That's no way to start a job. Their strategy worked. I called the next day and said I couldn't take the job.

I liked Woestendiek. He was a good guy. They fired him two years later and he became a director of the University of Southern California journalism school. He was in Cleveland for only three years. I don't think it was a happy experience.

So I concentrated on my new full-time career as a sports reporter at Channel 8. Eventually, they threw me in front of the camera as an anchor. Let me put it this way. Even the Titanic had an anchor.

Acknowledgements

So many people to thank, so little time.

To the Living:
Chuck Murr, my personal editor.
Eugene McCormick and Julie McCormick, who helped launch the
    project.
John Davis for invaluable business advice.
Bill Wynne for sharing his photographs.
Dino Lucarelli and Bob DiBiasio, two guys who know how to
    make friends and influence people. The last of a breed.
Jackie York for Dime Beer Night.
Doug Dieken for mirrors on the ceiling.
Les Levine, the voice of truth and reason.
Arnold Miller, the classic small town managing editor.
Dan Garvey for fixing my car; David Jonke and the late Farrell
    Gallagher for fixing my teeth; Inderjit Gill for fixing my heart;
    Judge Seamus F.X. Corrigan for fixing my tickets.
The Plain Dealer for 18 wonderful years and for allowing me to
    reprint a dozen columns and parts of three others.
The *Cleveland Press* Archives at Cleveland State University and
    archivists William C. Barrow and Lynn M. Duchez Bycko.
The *Elyria Chronicle-Telegram, Medina Gazette, Lake County
    News-Herald, Dayton Daily News* and *Ashtabula Star-Beacon*
    for providing a pulpit.

May They Rest in Peace:
My grandmother, Frances Strain, and my mother, Ruth Coughlin,
    who stressed erudition and tolerance in our house.
Sister Aurelia, C.S.J., who taught me to diagram sentences
    or die.
Hal Lebovitz, an editor who improved everything I wrote.
Joe Cole, who put the Coughlin family in a bigger house.
Gil Rosenwald, who launched my radio career at WHK.

Dick Zunt, my dearest friend and answer man who never forgot a
  name.
Bartenders Nino Rinicella and Walter Kulon.
Avenues Magazine, the *Cleveland Press, Cleveland News, Paines-
  ville Telegraph* and *Cableviews*. Gone but not forgotten.

About the Author

Dan Coughlin has covered the Cleveland sports scene for 45 years
as a newspaperman, magazine writer, television broadcaster and
radio commentator. He was twice named Ohio sportswriter of the
year and was honored with a television Emmy. He traveled with both
the Cleveland Browns and Indians. He covered some of the biggest
college football games of the 20th century, including five major bowl
games. As a boxing writer he was at ringside for several world championship fights as well as the Muhammad Ali and Joe Frazier series.
He covered 17 Indianapolis 500s and several auto races in Europe.
While in college he broadcast Notre Dame basketball and baseball
games on the student radio station.

  Dan served his alma mater, St. Edward High School, as a member
of its board of trustees for 20 years. Because of his generosity,
several bartenders were able to send their sons to St. Edward. He is
a member of the Greater Cleveland Softball Hall of Fame and the
Press Club of Cleveland Hall of Fame, and he is a past president of
the Press Club. He now lives in Rocky River, Ohio, with his wife,
Maddy.

OTHER BOOKS OF INTEREST . . .

Just One More Story . . .
A Last Batch of Stories About the Most Unusual, Eccentric and Outlandish People I've Known in Five Decades as a Sports Journalist

Dan Coughlin

This fourth batch of humorous tales from Cleveland sports journalist Dan Coughlin includes a Pro Bowl left tackle who would try anything once (including being a state senator), the priest who got himself ejected from a baseball game, Art Modell's attempt at high culture in Municipal Stadium, and a school teacher obsessed with making free throws.

Pass the Nuts
More Stories About The Most Unusual, Eccentric & Outlandish People I've Known in Four Decades as a Sports Journalist

Dan Coughlin

A second rollicking collection of tales about colorful characters and memorable events from the author of "Crazy, With the Papers to Prove It." Sportswriter Dan Coughlin has met everyone from gun-toting softball fanatics to millionaire sports team owners. Reading his stories is like dipping into a bowl of bar nuts—easy to start and hard to stop!

"A trove of tales—some poignant, even tragic; many hilarious." – Akron Beacon Journal

Let's Have Another
Even More Stories About the Most Unusual, Eccentric & Outlandish People I've Known in Four Decades as a Sports Journalist

Dan Coughlin

This third batch of humorous stories from Cleveland sports journalist Dan Coughlin includes a nutty team owner who nearly killed his franchise (and some spectators), an adventurous Browns lineman who survived a gunshot wound, an Indians slugger with the worst attitude in baseball, a brilliant tennis promoter who "stole" the Davis Cup, and others.

Read samples at **www.grayco.com**

OTHER BOOKS OF INTEREST . . .

The Best of Hal Lebovitz
Great Sportswriting from Six Decades in Cleveland

Hal Lebovitz

The best sports writing of Hal Lebovitz, the dean of Cleveland sportswriters for six decades. Many of his columns were anthologized in "Best American Sportswriting" and other collections, and he won countless national and regional sportswriting awards—among them induction into the writers' wing of the National Baseball Hall of Fame.

"A Hall of Fame writer at the top of his game." – The Beacon Journal

Joe Tait: It's Been a Real Ball
Stories from a Hall-of-Fame Sports Broadcasting Career

Terry Pluto, Joe Tait

Legendary broadcaster Joe Tait is like an old family friend to three generations of Cleveland sports fans. This book celebrates the inspiring career of "the Voice of the Cleveland Cavaliers" with stories from Joe and dozens of fans, colleagues, and players. Hits the highlights of a long career and also uncovers some touching personal details.

"An easy, fun book to read and will surely bring back good memories for Cleveland sports fans who listened to Tait's trademark calls since 1970." – 20SecondTimeout.com

Gimme Rewrite, Sweetheart
Tales From the Last Glory Days of Cleveland Newspapers—Told By The Men and Women Who Reported the News

John H. Tidyman

Listen in as dozens of veteran newspaper reporters, editors, and photographers swap favorite tales about life on the job at Cleveland's newspapers in the 1950s, '60s, and '70s—when fierce competition made daily newspapers the most exciting business in town. Funny, tragic, sometimes outrageous, it's a boisterous look at "the first draft of history."

"Utterly fascinating . . . highly recommended anyone curious about heyday of newspapers." – Library Book Watch

Read samples at **www.grayco.com**